Lalla Ward's
COUNTRYSIDE EMBROIDERY BOOK

LALLA WARD'S
Countryside Embroidery Book

Photography by Tony Evans

PELHAM BOOKS

Stephen Greene Press

PELHAM BOOKS

Published by the Penguin Group
27 Wrights Lane, London W8 5TZ, England
Viking Penguin Inc., 40 West 23rd Street, New York, New York 10010,
USA
The Stephen Greene Press, 15 Muzzey Street, Lexington,
Massachusetts 02173, USA
Penguin Books Australia Ltd, Ringwood, Victoria, Australia
Penguin Books Canada Ltd, 2801 John Street, Markham, Ontario,
Canada L3R 1B4
Penguin Books (NZ) Ltd, 182-190 Wairau Road, Auckland 10,
New Zealand

Penguin Books Ltd, Registered Offices:
Harmondsworth, Middlesex, England

First published 1989

Typeset in 10/11pt Clearface Regular by
Goodfellow & Egan Phototypesetting Ltd, Cambridge
Colour reproduction by Anglia Graphics, Bedford
Printed and bound in Spain by Cayfosa Industria Grafica, Barcelona

A CIP catalogue for this book is available from the British Library

ISBN 0 7207 1853 8

For Bill Gibb

Contents

Embroideries

Acknowledgements

I think I would like, first and foremost, to thank myself for spending hours and hours and hours embroidering every stitch in this book! Seriously, though . . . none of it would have been possible without the enthusiasm and encouragement of the following:

My wonderful agent Heather Jeeves.

Jeremy Hawtrey-Woore at the Royal Society for the Protection of Birds, who put up with all my bullying and let me do the calendar for 1990, from which all the embroideries in this book are taken.

Roger Houghton, who has been the best editor anyone could ask for, always on the same wavelength and never nagging me about deadlines!

Tony Evans, who took such care to produce photographs which really do look so like the actual embroideries that you could almost touch them and feel the threads.

Liz Elvin and the workshop at the Royal School of Needlework, who mounted all the work for me and didn't faint with horror at my somewhat unorthodox methods! I was so frightened when I first went to see them at their Hampton Court establishment, thinking that they would find me the most hopeless amateur and send me packing, and they were all so nice and enthusiastic. Thank you, Liz, for all your help.

Ailsa Green, who used to work at the Royal School of Needlework, and who gave me lots of good advice when I first started the calendar and book.

Diana Springall, who has been so kind and helpful whenever I have telephoned her with some problem.

Harriet Evans, for testing my stitch instructions to see if they were really easy to understand.

DMC Dunlicraft and Cara Whigham, for their help.

All my friends who put up with me taking my needlework with me to dinner parties, week-ends, whatever, just to get the horrendous amount of work done in time. I've hardly looked at anyone who's been talking to me in the year it's taken to complete work on this book, and I've left little bits of coloured thread all over the sofas and tables of their houses. Especial thanks to my parents, to Gloria and Michael Birkett and to Joanna David for their encouragement, and to my little niece Anna, for inspiring me to make the 'Anna' sampler.

My darling friend Bill Gibb, to whom this book is dedicated and who died, tragically, at the beginning of 1988. He always gave me so much encouragement and I miss him dreadfully.

Introduction

I hate sewing. When I was little I took two whole school terms to make an apron which was so hideous that I never wore it or dared give it to anyone and the sorry experience put me off sewing forever. I'm still hopeless at hems and buttonholes and would rather go barefoot than have to darn a sock. Embroidery isn't sewing. I want to persuade the other failed apron-makers of this world that this is something altogether different, a new way of making pictures, and that it should be enjoyable, not a gruesome chore.

It seems to be a popular feeling at the moment that technique is a bit of a bore and that if you can get away with knowing just one stitch, then that's wonderful. My thinking is exactly the opposite. I love the business of learning new stitches, of making the character of the stitch itself an important part of the picture. These embroideries are about form and texture, not just colour, and I want the learning of the techniques involved to be exciting. I hope that once you have mastered a stitch and used it to arrive at a particular effect, you will feel a sense of achievement and have enjoyed the whole process.

All that said, there are some things to do with technique that I find desperately boring. I'm sure that I shall enrage the purists, but this was always meant to be a very personal approach and there are lots of books written for purists.

I really don't mind if lines are not all that straight or if you can't cope with the stitch that I've suggested and want to substitute one that you find easier. Your way may be better. For instance, I've stuck to fairly simple ideas for the borders of each picture, but if you already know other interesting border stitches, then use them instead. I don't care what the back of the embroidery looks like either. No-one will see it once it has been framed or made into a cushion or whatever, and yet it is amazing how, whenever someone looks at your work, the first thing they do is turn it over to see what a mess you have made of the under side. What on earth does it matter? What does matter is that you should enjoy yourself making the embroidery, not that you should have a breakdown worrying about whether you should start off with a knot or not, or whether you can get away with a horrible tangle on the wrong side that would only ever be seen by some nosey-parker anyway.

When I started this book, I'd managed to get to grips with three or four of the really simple stitches, like Stem and Satin. I learnt more of them as I went along and the thing that I found most difficult was understanding the various instruction books with which I taught myself. They seemed to be written from the point of view of someone who was perfectly used to the stitch and who had long since forgotten what it was like to try and master it for the very first time. I found that I could get half way through working out some horrible little brute and then the instructions, rather like road signs, suddenly gave up explaining the route and left me stranded. I've written and illustrated my own instructions for every stitch used in this book and tried really hard to show you as clearly as possible how the process is done. It seems to me that this vitally important part of embroidery is so often crammed into a corner of a book as if it might be embarrassing to give more than a stingy line or two to describing something that, to a beginner, can be as obscure as a foreign language. I've probably gone too far the other way and over-explained every little detail, but I think it is a fault in the right direction. Learning a new stitch should be fun in itself, not drive you to drink and despair.

I've used a technique rather like something called stump work, if you know what that is . . . it seems to have gone out of fashion, but was used for things such as coats of arms, where padding parts of the picture made them stand out from the background. It's a wonderful effect, not difficult to achieve and I hope I have explained as clearly and simply as possible how to do it.

I practiced new stitches by making up the sampler pictures illustrated here. (Anna is my

gorgeous little niece and I thought that it would be nice to combine practice with something to give her when it was finished . . . it's a good incentive to try hard!) It's much more fun than embroidering row after row of boring stitches just for the sake of it. Make a simple little drawing of anything: copy something from a book, make a picture of your cat or a plant or copy roughly what I have done. Keep your sampler small so that you haven't given yourself a massive chore to finish it. Mine are tiny, just four or five inches (10–13 cm) square, or four by six inches (10 x 15 cm) . . . enough room to get good at as many stitches as you want to cram into the space. I learnt a lot from my mistakes. Some of the stitches that I'd struggled with weren't necessarily any better than other, simpler alternatives. I weeded out the horrendously difficult ones. I didn't see why you should have to tackle them if they had defeated me.

Read the chapter on General Know-How and read through the instructions for a particular picture before you start, just as you would a cooking recipe. It will help, even if you are experienced, to have a rough idea of what I'm getting at before you launch yourself into the work itself.

Each one of the twelve pictures represents one month of a Royal Society for the Protection of Birds calendar for 1990. The photographs, Detailed Outlines and Key Diagrams are the actual size of the finished pictures, to help you.

You can frame your work, or use it for the central panel of a cushion, or take a detail such as a bumble-bee or a single bird and embroider it onto the lapel or pocket of a jacket. It's entireiy up to you.

Please don't be put off if you are a complete beginner, and feel that you couldn't possibly tackle one of these pictures. You can. I did. And I had to do all twelve of them, so you can at least have a go at one and you may very well discover that, once you've started, you will want to go on and do another . . . and if you are experienced, you will probably do a much better job than I did and can feel really pleased with yourself!

The most important thing, whether you are experienced or a beginner like me, is to enjoy yourself.

General know-how

EQUIPMENT YOU WILL NEED

Fabric
Scissors
A waterproof felt-tip pen
Tracing paper
An embroidery ring or frame
Needles
Threads
A thimble
Felt
Blotting paper
Mounting card, fine string and fabric glue
Patience

GETTING STARTED

Fabric

I've used a mixture of linen and cotton which I got from Liberty in Regent Street, London. Almost any fabric with a firm, more or less even weave will do and the choice is enormous. Pure linen is expensive and I like the slightly lighter weight of the cotton/linen mixture. Synthetics are cheaper still, but I find they feel rather nasty to work on and offend my fashionable craving for the natural. The best thing is to go into a large department store like Liberty or John Lewis, or go to a specialist shop, or you can get all sorts of supplies from the Royal School of Needlework's mail order service (see List of Suppliers, page 128).

Scissors

You will need a pair of small, pointed, sharp embroidery scissors, and a pair of large scissors for cutting out your fabric.

Transferring the Design onto Fabric

Use the Detailed Outline, which is the size of the actual embroidery, so you won't need to enlarge or reduce it. You could make the picture bigger if you were a real devil for punishment and hard work, in which case there are lots of embroidery books which tell you how to do so, but I think this size is ideal and I should stick to it unless you want to get into terrible dramas about how much extra thread you are going to need and so on.

Cut out your fabric so that it is at least two inches (5 cm) larger all round than the Detailed Outline, in other words, a good 11 inches (28 cm) square. I tend to leave far more spare than that because you can always trim it down later, but to have too little is miserable when it comes to mounting the work.

It helps to hem around the edges to avoid fraying. If I'm feeling really lazy, I just stick masking tape over the edges. Disgusting, I know, but you've already discovered how much I hate sewing!

Make a tracing of the Detailed Outline, using your permanent, indelible waterproof pen. Please, please, don't be tempted to use the non-waterproof kind. When you come to dampen the work for stretching, it would be tragic if your drawing were to run and ruin all the hours of work. I used an Edding 2104 permanent, which is 'water and rub-proof instant dry' and ideal. You can get it from artists' supply shops, but there are lots of good alternatives to be found in ordinary stationers. Just be sure to check that it really is waterproof.

Stick this tracing up onto a window pane. Stick your fabric on top of the tracing and lo and behold, you have an instant light box. The daylight will shine through the tracing and the fabric (don't try doing this at night, and a sunny day helps!) You will now be able to see the Detailed Outline and trace it directly onto your fabric. I know it feels a bit odd drawing on a vertical surface and of course an actual light box would be the ideal, but most of us don't have such esoteric equipment and this is a very good alternative. There are other ways of transferring a design and if you prefer them, by all means use them; this just happens to be the way which I find the easiest.

Embroidery Ring

You can do some kinds of embroidery without keeping the work taut and smooth in a frame or ring, but for this particular method it would be pretty well impossible. The fabric must be taut when you come to padding sections of the design and a lot of the stitches used would be very difficult to do without the tension of the surface being maintained.

There are lots of rings on the market. A ten inch (25 cm) ring is ideal for this work, although you can, of course, lace it to a square frame if you prefer. I found the kind of ring that attaches to a table, or fits into a stand, to be quite good, but, necessity being the clichéd mother of invention, I made my life even easier by coming up with the brilliant alternative which is illustrated here. This is a wonderfully versatile version of the ordinary ring and enables you to change position as often as you like, even to work slouched back in a comfortable armchair, and to avoid what I found to be a torture of working hour after hour, the inevitable backache that comes from being forced to stay for too long in one position. My embroidery ring invention will be available at selected shops by the time this book is on the market and I sincerely recommend it if you do a lot of embroidery. It will have a ten inch (25 cm) ring and will have a magnifier attachment for those of you who find the work terribly hard on the eyes. Both hands are free and you will find it really does make life considerably easier.

I found that by binding the inner ring, I could protect the fabric and that it was gripped better between the two rings.

Adjust the screw so that the outer ring fits easily but not too loosely over the inner ring and then remove the outer ring. Lay your fabric over the inner ring, centering the transferred Detailed Outline, and press the outer ring firmly down over the fabric, then tighten the screw. The fabric should be absolutely taut. If it isn't remove the outer ring and start again, don't loosen the screw and tug at the fabric or you will only distort the weave.

Needles

Stranded cotton is very versatile. You can use anything from all six strands at once down to just a single strand. You can mix colours, using, say two strands of light green with one strand of a darker shade, threaded into the same needle, to give wonderfully subtle shading effects. It might seem an awful bore, but having the right size and type of needle for the job really does make an enormous difference. Using an ordinary, sharp needle for a stitch like Detached Overcast, for example, is a nightmare of catching the fabric and splitting the foundation stitches, whereas if you take the trouble to change to a blunt-ended tapestry needle, the job is quite simple. For all of your work with Stranded Cotton, use Milward Embroidery Crewel needles in the following sizes:

Number 8 for one or two strands
Number 7 for three strands
Number 6 for four strands
Number 5 for six strands

Where I have suggested you use a blunt-ended needle for interlacing or overcasting, use Milward Tapestry needles. I used Number 24 for one, two, three and four strands and Number 20 for five and six strands.

I used a Milward Chenille needle, Number 20, for padding with bump (see the section on Threads below). These are sharp needles with big eyes.

I found it helpful to write out these needle and thread combinations on a card so that I could refer to them easily, since I never seemed to be able to remember whether I should be using a number 7 or 6 or whatever with which number of strands. It saves an awful lot of rummaging back through the book each time you change needles.

Threads

Almost all the threads used in this book are made by DMC. There are other kinds available, but I found these to have the most beautiful colours and texture. All the stranded cottons are from their enormous range and I've used their lovely Soft Cotton, rather unglamourously, for padding. It's far too beautiful, really, to be used for such a task, but is the perfect weight and texture. See the specific instructions for Padding with Felt and Bump (page 39).

I've used DMC's Silver Divisible, which comes in a spool, for things like icicles. One spool will be far more than enough even if you were to work every single picture in this book.

The only threads I've used which aren't made by DMC are the other, coloured, metallic threads. These are made by Elizabeth Stuart and come in a range of truly gorgeous colours. They are expensive and I've given stranded cotton alternatives if you don't feel like being extravagant. If you do, they should be available from the Royal School of Needlework's mail order service (see List of Suppliers, page 128) and from other specialist shops.

Felt

Felt can be bought in squares, eight and a half inches by eight and a half inches (22 x 22 cm), from the haberdashery departments of stores like John Lewis. You will need it for padding. It's a good idea to have a neutral colour like beige and perhaps a darker colour, for padding darker areas. One square of each will be ample for just one picture, although you might like to have a bit more in stock in case you go on and do more. You can buy felt by the metre, too, if you find it an easier way. Have a good look at the specific instructions for Padding with Felt and Bump (page 39) before starting this operation.

FINISHING OFF

Blotting Paper

You may find that you do not have to stretch your finished embroidery, but if you do, then this is the way that Diana Springall told me was the best, and has described in her lovely book, *Design for Embroidery*:

Start by laying several sheets of blotting paper onto a drawing board, or wooden surface.

Wet the blotting paper thoroughly with water. Don't try and wet the blotting paper first and then put it on the board, you will be struggling with a horrible, soggy mess.

Lay your work face up on the wet blotting paper.

Starting at the centre of one edge, gently but firmly press in drawing pins at about 1 inch (2–3 cm) intervals. As Diana says, the pins must be secure, but don't bash them with a hammer or the spikes will simply part company with the heads.

Pull the opposite side of the work to straighten it and put drawing pins along this edge.

Treat the other two sides in the same way, until there are no wrinkles left.

Leave it to dry overnight and then remove the pins.

Mounting Card, Fine String and Fabric Glue

Now you can mount your work, if you are going to frame it. Cut out a piece of Daler mounting board, stiff cardboard or thin hardboard, to the size of the finished work, plus enough to fit under the frame rebate if you don't want it to overlap your work.

You can cover the board with fabric first, if you want a good, smooth finish. Cut out a square of your linen/cotton or whatever you used for the embroidery, or a piece of flannelette, if you have such a thing to hand, about an inch and a half (3–4 cm) bigger all round than your card. Apply thin strips of glue close to the edges on the wrong side of your mounting card.

Place the card, glue side up, onto the backing fabric and fold down the fabric neatly onto the glue.

Allow the glue to dry properly.

Now centre the mounting card on the wrong side of your embroidery, turn over the edges and lace them, as illustrated.

When you come to having the work framed, I think it's a pity to cover such a tactile object with glass. It's up to you, of course.

As I've already said in the Introduction, you could use these embroideries to form the central panel of a cushion, or you could take a detail from any one of the designs, such as a bumble-bee or individual bird, and embroider it onto a garment. There are lots of books to tell you how to make cushions so I shan't go into the whole subject here and, if you want to add a detail to a ready made garment, I think the easiest way is to do the embroidery on a matching, separate piece of fabric, cut it out carefully, turn under the edges and appliqué it onto the garment, on a lapel or pocket or collar.

Patience

You will need quite a lot of this.

LACING YOUR WORK OVER MOUNTING CARD

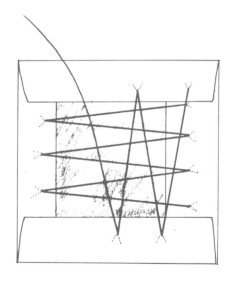

Stitch instructions

I've given illustrated instructions for all the stitches used in this book. Some of them, like Stem stitch and Satin stitch, are used in every one of the twelve embroideries. Sometimes I have used a stitch in just one picture, like Sorbello stitch for one of the January borders.

There are eighteen actual stitches plus instructions for Padding with Felt and Bump and Using Metal Thread.

When you have decided upon which picture you want to make, have a look through the list of Stitches You Will Need to Know. If you don't know any of them, then study the instructions carefully, get yourself a spare piece of material and practice, so that when you come to the picture itself, you are comfortable with all the stitches needed to complete it.

You could do as I suggested in the introduction, and make a little practice picture. It really is more fun than embroidering rows that will never be used for anything. None of these stitches is really difficult to learn, so don't despair before you've even started. I hope that the instructions and illustrations will help you and not tie you in miserable knots! I know just how frustrating it can be to try and understand someone else's methods and I have done my very best to make them as clear as possible.

You will find practice easier if you use a light rather than a dark coloured thread. It's awfully hard to see what you are doing with the very dark colours . . . and awfully helpful later on, since you can't see the mistakes as clearly, either!

Take your time. Try not to get into a state if you don't succeed immediately. Some of the more involved stitches look pretty terrible until you have finished enough of a line or section for them to come together. Don't despair and do try to see the funny side if you make a complete hash of it! You'll soon be in control of the situation.

The stitches suggested in the specific instructions for each picture are just that: suggestions. I've used what I felt to be the best ones for the job but if you have other ideas of your own, please feel free to try them out. And if you are especially unhappy with any of them, don't make your life wretched. Use something that you find easier. The bord-ers, for example, are made up for the most part of fairly uncomplicated stitches. I've used a Striped Woven Band in the June picture, but if you hate working it, use some other border stitch. Or put it into one of the other pictures, if you are particularly fond of it. Stick to the colour scheme of the picture and do remember that different stitches use up different amounts of thread and that you may need more or less than I have allowed for if you chop and change. The amount of thread needed is always difficult to calculate since, just as in knitting, we all work at different tensions and are slightly more or slightly less wasteful. I have tried always to allow enough in each 'recipe', but one can never be absolutely precise.

BEGINNING AND FINISHING OFF

When you use an embroidery ring it is easier to keep all of the work on the surface. It would be maddening to have to turn it over every time you begin or finish off. Start by making a small knot in your thread. It's much the simplest method and will never be seen once your picture is mounted or turned into a cushion. Finish off with two or three tiny back stitches on the front within a shape that will be embroidered over as you go along. Snip the thread off on the right side of your work.

BULLION KNOT

Bullion knots take a bit of practice to get good at and can be rather fiddly and maddening even when you've built up a bit of confidence. Trying to make too long a knot, with more than six or seven twists to it, is asking for tears and bad-temper.

I've used this stitch for the hedgehog's prickles.

Fig.1 Bring the needle through to the front of the fabric at A and insert at B.

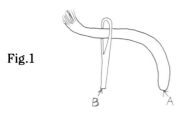

Fig.1

Fig.2 Leaving a loop, as illustrated, bring the needle half way through at A again.

Fig.2

Fig.3 Hold the needle from below the fabric with your right hand and, with your left hand, twist the thread around the needle point until the number of twists (six or seven at the most, but start with smaller, four or five twist knots for practice) will fill up the distance between A and B when the knot lies flat on the fabric.

Now comes the tricky bit; hold the needle point and the thread twisted around it lightly but firmly between the left thumb and forefinger.

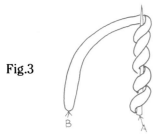

Fig.3

Fig.4 With the right hand, pull the needle through the twists until the knot lies flat between points A and B. Don't

try to do this bit too quickly or you will end up with a tangled mess. Once the knot is lying flat you can use the point of the needle to ease any bumps and snaggles in the twists.

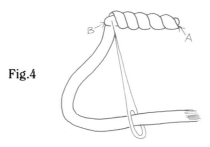

Fig.4

Fig.5 Insert the needle at B again and pull through gently to the back of the fabric to finish off.

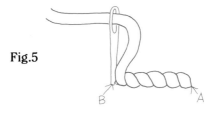

Fig.5

Don't get cross if it takes a bit of time to master these little brutes. It's a great effect in the end and worth the effort.

CHINESE KNOT

I personally prefer this knot to the better known French variety. It's flatter and neater and very easy to do and was used a lot in the gorgeous silk embroideries of China. I've used a single knot to add a highlight to the eyes of almost all the creatures in this book, and sometimes to cover a padded area, like the snow in the January picture.

Fig.1 Bring the needle through at A. Make a loop as illustrated and insert the needle at B.

Tighten the loop around the needle and hold down on the fabric with your left thumb as you pull the needle through, to keep the knot in place.

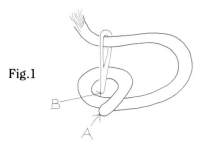

Fig.1

DETACHED CHAIN STITCH

These are just single links of ordinary chain stitch (see Interlaced Chain stitch, page 24).

Fig.1   Make the first, looped stitch, by bringing the needle through to the front of the fabric at A and inserting it again at A, leaving a small loop. Fix this loop, or link, of the chain in place, as you would at the end of a line of chain stitch, by bringing the needle through the front again at B and inserting it at C, to form a small, anchoring stitch.

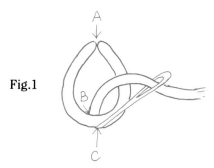

Fig.1

Fig.2   Just work individual links in this way, at random or, as for the fishes scales, all lying sideways to look as if each link in this case represents a scale. Very easy.

Fig.2

DETACHED OVERCAST STITCH

This stitch is wonderful for the kind of tendrils that trail over one another or an obstacle of some sort, and for birds' feet where they go over a branch. I must say that it is not my favourite stitch to work but it does achieve one of my favourite effects so I grit my teeth and bear with the fiddlesomeness of it all . . . it's not difficult, just tiresome.

Fig.1   Follow the line of the tendril or bird's foot or whatever, from point A to point B with a foundation line of long stem stitches.

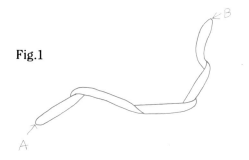

Fig.1

Fig.2   Now make a second foundation line of stem stitch, again starting at point A and finishing at point B, (shaded blue in the illustration) following exactly the same route as the first line but picking up the ground fabric at different places.

Don't try to get away with just one line of foundation stitches. The overcasting won't work on a single line foundation because you would get stuck where the stem stitch picks up the ground fabric. Having two lines that pick up the fabric in different places means that the overcast stitch has a loose foundation thread to go over at all times.

Fig.2

Fig.3   Now bring the needle through to the front of the fabric again at A and begin the overcasting stitch, as illustrated, being careful not to pick up any of the ground fabric. You will find it much easier if you switch to a blunt-ended tapestry needle.

Take care to keep the overcast stitches close together and pick up both lines of foundation stitches except where one enters the fabric.

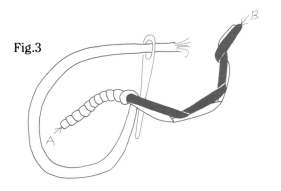

Fig.3

INTERLACED CHAIN STITCH

This makes a lovely solid border. I've used it for the October picture, but if you especially like it, there's really no reason why you shouldn't use it for one of the borders in any of the other pictures. See how you feel.

This stitch is not nearly as hard to do as it looks, you'll be pleased to know! It's far, far easier to work than the complicated illustration was to draw, I promise you! That was a real nightmare.

Fig.1   Start by making a line of ordinary chain stitch, as illustrated, bringing the needle through to the front of the fabric at A and, holding the thread down with your left hand, inserting the needle again at A.

Make a loop and bring the needle through to the front again at B, keeping this first loop under the thread as you pull the thread through.

Fig.1

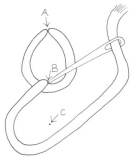

Insert the needle at B again, make another loop and bring the needle through to the front again at C . . . and so on until you reach the end of your line. Fix the last loop as though you were going to carry on but, instead of making another loop, taking the needle back into the fabric to form a little anchoring stitch (at B in Fig.2).

Fig.2   Use a contrasting coloured thread (shaded black on the illustration) and switch to a blunt-ended tapestry needle. You will need to have enough thread in your needle to make it all the way to the end of the chain without having to re-thread. I found that you actually need about four times the length of the chain line to get comfortably to the end without panicking that you are going to run out. It's a bit on the extravagant side but better than running out halfway along.

Bring the needle through to the front of the fabric at A.

Take it under the SECOND link of the chain and bring it back and under the FIRST link and itself, as illustrated. Take care not to pick up any of the ground fabric. The ONLY times you take the needle through the fabric on this interlacing journey are at point A at the beginning of the chain and point B at the end.

Fig.2

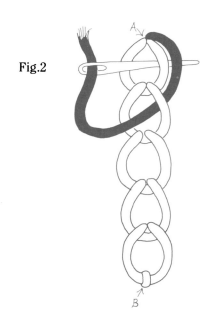

Fig.3   Take the needle under the THIRD link and back under the SECOND link and itself, as illustrated.

Fig.3

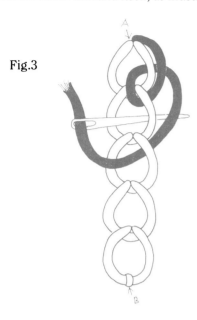

Fig.4   Continue in this way until you get to the end of the chain and then insert the needle at B, take the thread to the back of the fabric and finish off.

Fig.4

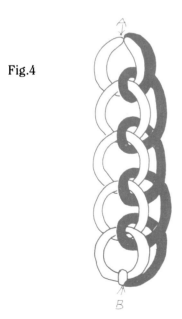

Fig.5   Now start again at the top, again threading your blunt-ended needle with enough of the same colour (contrasting with the chain line) to get safely to the end and working your way down the left hand side of the chain. For the sake of clarity, I've shaded this side in little dots, so you can see how it goes.

When you get to the end of the chain line, finish off just as before.

Fig.5

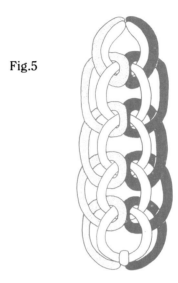

OVERCAST STITCH

This is really just an easier version of Detached Overcast (page 23). I've used it in between Detached Overcast, where branches or whatever don't actually need to trail over anything and can happily be attached to the fabric.

Fig.1

Fig.1   First make a line of running stitches (shaded black in the illustration) and then cover these little stitches with small, straight stitches worked at right angles. The needle should pick up only the tiniest amount of fabric as it makes each stitch. If you pick up too much ground fabric, your overcast line won't be nice and rounded.

PORTUGUESE KNOTTED STEM STITCH

Have a look at the instructions for ordinary Stem stitch (page 35) and practise it if it is a stitch with which you are unfamiliar. It's very simple and the Portuguese variety is really not all that complicated, although it does take longer to work.

It's a lovely, knobbly stitch for filling in branches, for example, and, although you are meant to make two knots around each stem stitch, I have sometimes only made one to vary the effect and make some of the stitches less knobbly.

Fig.1   Make your first stitch, just as in ordinary Stem stitch, from point A to point B.

Make the second, again just as in ordinary Stem stitch, from point C to point D. Come through to the front again at point B, just as if you were going to make another ordinary Stem stitch, but this time slide your needle UNDER the first two stitches, as illustrated, being very careful NOT to go into the fabric at all. Pull the thread through carefully. This forms your first Portuguese Knot.

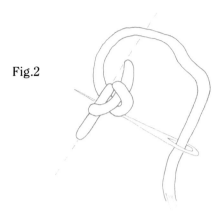

Fig.2

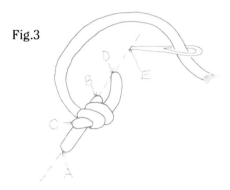

Fig.3   Now insert the needle at E, just as you would to make another ordinary Stem stitch.

Fig.3

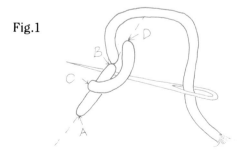

Fig.1

Fig.2   Take the needle UNDER the first two stitches yet again, being very careful not to go into the fabric at all. Pull the thread through gently. This forms the second Portuguese Knot.

Fig.4   Bring the needle through to the front again at D (I've moved further along the line to show you how it will eventually look) and now make another two Portuguese Knots around this Stem stitch, just as before, again being careful not to go into the fabric.

You will find that you get to grips with this stitch quite easily. Where it is worked in rows to fill a space, do so in such a way as to avoid getting your needle caught in the previous row as you work the knots, in other words starting along the top row of a horizontal branch and working your way down it row after row rather than the other way around, where every previous row would lie directly in the line of your needle as you slip it under the Stem stitches. You will see immediately what I am getting at as you work a row or two.

Fig.4

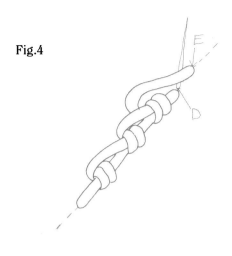

Fig.2   Bring the needle through to the front again at G and insert again at H. Bring the needle through to the front again at I and insert again at J.

Fig.2

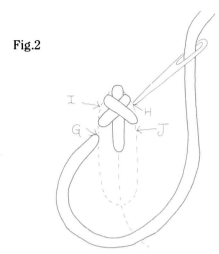

RAISED FISHBONE STITCH

This stitch looks far more complicated than it is. It makes a nice, fat shape that is useful for filling in leaves and feathers, if not necessarily fish.

Fig.1   Bring the thread through to the front of the fabric at A. Insert the needle at B, about half way down the centre line of the shape.
Bring the needle through the front again at C.
Insert again at D.
Bring the needle through to the front again at E.
Insert the needle again at F.

Fig.3   And so on . . . so that each time, you are making a diagonal stitch on the surface and a horizontal one underneath the work, building up slanting and crossing stitches until you have covered the whole shape, Fig.4.

Fig.3

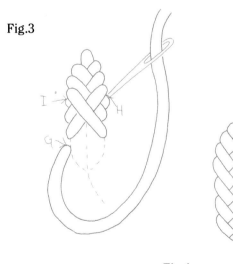

Fig.1

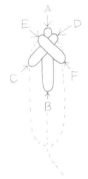

Fig.4

ROPE STITCH

This is rather like Satin stitch (page 29) except that it's raised up on one side by the twist of the thread. I've used it for the Barn Owl's wing in the August picture, and for one of the August borders.

I can't understand a word of the usual explanations for this stitch; I tied myself and my thread in bad-tempered knots trying to get to grips with what is, in fact, really quite an easy stitch. Either I'm terribly thick or have a peculiar way of working things out ... If you find my explanations incomprehensible, try another book. We may just be on different wavelengths!

Fig.1   Following the outline from right to left, bring the needle through to the front of the fabric at A and insert again at B.

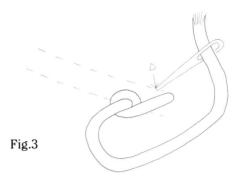

Fig.3

Fig.4   Emerge again at E, loop the thread around the needle as before and pull through so that the second stitch lies next to the first.

Fig.1

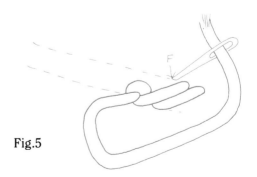

Fig.4

Fig.5   Insert the needle again at F. And so on along the line. Keep a good slant, inserting and bringing the needle through very close to the previous stitch so that the twist underneath doesn't show through.

Fig.2   Emerge again at C and, holding the thread with your left hand, loop it around the needle as illustrated.

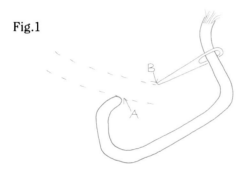

Fig.2

Fig.5

Fig.3   Pull the thread through and insert the needle again at D.

ROUMANIAN COUCHING

This is a useful stitch for filling in large spaces. I've used it a lot to cover the padding of an animal or bird's body.

Fig.1   Bring the needle through to the front at A and insert at B, thus laying a long thread from one side to the other of the shape you want to cover.

Fig.1

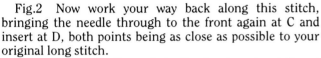

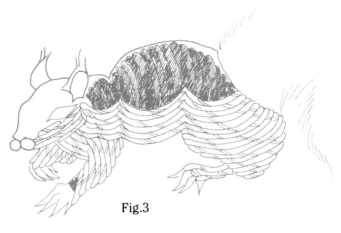

Fig.3

Fig.2   Now work your way back along this stitch, bringing the needle through to the front again at C and insert at D, both points being as close as possible to your original long stitch.

Bring the needle through to the front again at E and insert again at F. And so on along the line, making as many of these couching stitches as you need to keep the original long stitch in place. They should be angled in such a way as to be as invisible as possible.

SATIN STITCH

This is one of those sneaky stitches that looks as if it is going to be really easy and actually needs a bit of practice to work well. You can fill a shape with straight or slanting stitches.

Satin stitch is no good for filling in too large a shape, because the stitches would be too long and loose and get bedraggled, but it's immensely useful for all sorts of little shapes and I've used it all over the place.

Fig.1   For straight Satin stitch, come through to the front of the fabric at A and insert the needle at B, to form your first stitch and work your way along the line or within a shape, just like that. Couldn't be easier.

Fig.2

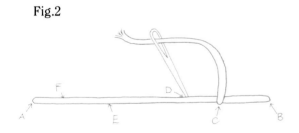

Fig.3   Cover the shape with row after row worked in the same way and laid close together. You can start anywhere along the edge of the shape. The couching stitches ensure the long, laid threads follow the contour of the padding.

The bump padding stitches are those shaded blue in the illustration.

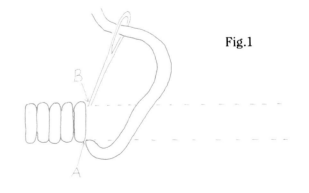

Fig.1

Fig.2 For the slanting variety, which, as illustrated, you can slant either way, again come through to the front at A and insert at B. The slightly tricky part (and really, it's only a matter of a bit of practice), is to maintain the slant of the stitches. For some curious reason, if you bring the needle through to the front and insert it both equally close to the previous stitch, your stitches will get gradually more vertical and straight. However, if you come through to the front (A on the illustration) just a fraction further away from the previous stitch and insert the needle at B, close to the previous stitch, and continue thus, you will maintain the slant. If the slant goes the other way, as on the top of the bird's head, the stitches at the bottom are close together and those at the top are spaced fractionally apart to maintain the slant in that direction.

You will get the hang of it quite quickly, once you have a bit of a practice.

Fig.2

SATIN STITCH COUCHING

The thread used for padding is, I am assured by the Royal School of Needlework, called 'bump'... bumping it up...?

You can use more or less any soft cotton for this job; I've used DMC's Soft Cotton which is a perfect thickness and texture for the purpose. It helps roughly to match the colour with which you will be covering this foundation padding. Use pale bump under pale Satin stitches and dark under dark Satin stitches... no matter how neat and tidy you are, a tiny bit might show through and it's much

harder work covering dark brown, say, with white, if like me, you are a bit slapdash and impatient to get on with it.

I've used this stitch a lot for the borders of each picture, laying two, three, four or five strands of bump, depending on how fat I want the border to be.

I'll use four strands for this particular explanation, but the technique is obviously the same however many are specified.

Start anywhere along the border unless specified in the instructions, preferably somewhere which will eventually have a leaf or something laid over it just in case, as is my little foible, you make a rather unglamorous join.

Cut off four strands of bump, each one long enough to reach from your starting point, all the way round the border and back to the starting point again, with a bit to spare for safety's sake.

Fig.1 Lay all four long threads of bump on the fabric (I haven't drawn the whole length in the diagram, obviously), bunching them on top of each other roughly to go along the line to be followed. You can bring the bump through from the back of the work but I think it's a lumpy, pointless exercise. Try to keep all the long trailing tail ends out of your way as you work. Now thread a needle with two or three strands (whichever is specified in the instructions) in the specified colour of stranded cotton.

Fig.1

Fig.2 Bring this couching thread (from the French *coucher*, to lay down), shaded blue in the diagram, through to the front of the fabric at A, leaving a half inch (1–2 cm) or so of the bump to be trimmed later.

Fig.2

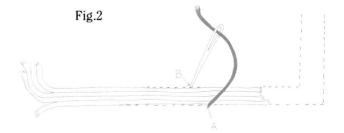

Insert the needle at B and form your first couching stitch, covering the bump and keeping it in place. You can slant the couching Satin stitches or make them straight, whichever you prefer.

Carry on thus all the way round the border, negotiating the corners as shown in Fig.3.

Fig.3   Work your way around until you are about an inch (2–3 cm) from where you started at point A. Trim both ends of the bump so as to be able to make as neat a join as possible and carry on covering with the couching stitches until no bump shows. Again, you can take the bump through to the back of the fabric if you want to but it isn't worth the effort and doesn't make the join any neater, in my opinion. See how you feel.

Other areas where I've used Satin Stitch Couching, such as the holly branches in the December picture, are worked in exactly the same way, cutting off enough bump for each little section.

Fig.3

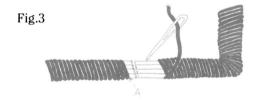

SEMI-DETACHED BUTTONHOLE

This is my version of what is supposed to be a completely Detached Buttonhole. You are supposed to work the stitch from left to right and then back again but I'm too stupid to work it backwards from right to left without getting into a bad-tempered tangle, so I've invented the Semi-Detached variation. If you want to do it the proper way, there are lots of books to tell you how; if you want to opt out and save your sanity, follow me.

There are two sections to these instructions, the first telling you how to do the stitch and the second showing you how specifically to put it into practice in the case of the August picture of the Barn Owl. I felt it was better to give this somewhat complicated bird a bit of space here so that you don't get in a muddle should you want to work it and because, in any case, it's a good example of the problems of Semi-Detached Buttonholing.

Section One

Fig.1   Start by making two foundation stitches down the centre of the shape from A to B.

Fig.1

Fig.2   Bring the needle through to the front again at A, then insert the needle under the two foundation stitches without picking up any of the fabric. Keep the thread under the needle, as illustrated, and pull tight, thus forming a buttonhole stitch attached to your foundation stitches.

Fig.2

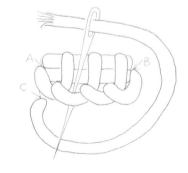

Fig.3   Make the next buttonhole stitch in exactly the same way and carry on to the end of the foundation line, being careful not to pick up any ground fabric.

Fig.3

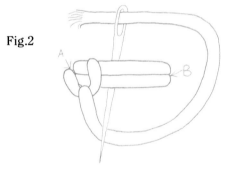

Fig.4   At the end of the line, insert the needle into the fabric at B and pull through to the back. Re-emerge at C.

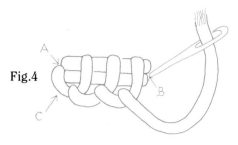

Fig.4

Fig.5   Work the next row into the loops formed by the previous row, again being careful not to pick up any of the ground fabric until you take the needle through to the back at the end of the row at D. Re-emerge at E and work the third row in exactly the same way, finishing by inserting the needle at F.

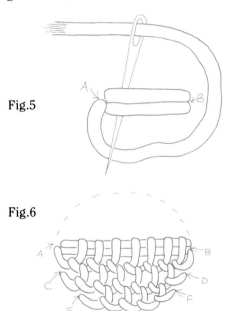

Fig.5

Fig.6

Work the other half of the shape in exactly the same way, laying down another two foundation stitches and working three rows of buttonhole over them. You will find it a million times easier if you turn the fabric around in the embroidery ring so that you are working in the same direction, unless you are a contortionist or unbelievably brilliant.

Some of the time you need only work two rows of buttonhole on each side, or for a really slim shape, just a single row.

You can change colours for each row, if you want to, as I have done for the November leaves. Just begin a new row with a new colour. Simple as that.

Section Two

Don't be put off by the incredible wordiness of these instructions . . . it's just that I really cannot think of a neater way to explain. Lots of it is pretty obvious, but I would rather, as usual, err on the side of over-explaining than leave you in the dark anywhere along the line. So bear with me.

It will help you if you turn your work around in the embroidery ring so that the owl is facing the way of these illustrations.

You will need to refer to the Key Diagram for August as well as the illustrations here and it wouldn't hurt to have a good look at the photograph to see what you are aiming for and then try and do it better than I did!

Fig.1   Start at F. Using two strands of 3047, lay two foundation stitches as indicated by the tiny dotted lines. Do the same at K, L, and M. These are your Semi-Detached Buttonhole foundation stitches.

Fig.2   Begin casting on the first row of Semi-Detached Buttonhole at F, using two strands of 3047 mixed with one strand of 680.

Carry on, covering the padding with row after row of Semi-Detached Buttonhole. You may find that you have to cast on an extra stitch at the beginning or end of a row, if there aren't enough to fill the space. You can do this easily, in a cheating sort of way, by making two buttonhole stitches into one of the stitches of the previous row. You can cast off in a similar way, if the space gets narrower and requires fewer stitches, simply by not adding a stitch into the starting or finishing stitch of the previous row.

Carry on until you reach your L foundation line and simply carry on along that row, casting on new stitches all along the foundation line to cope with the widening of the shape. It's really quite simple.

When you get to the interruption of the shoulder, at O on the illustration, you will have to stop and start on either side of the shoulder section, and carry on until you reach the heavy dotted lines, at P on the illustration.

STITCH INSTRUCTIONS

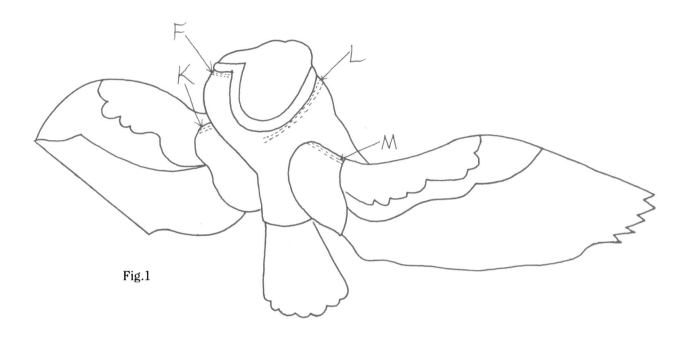

Fig.1

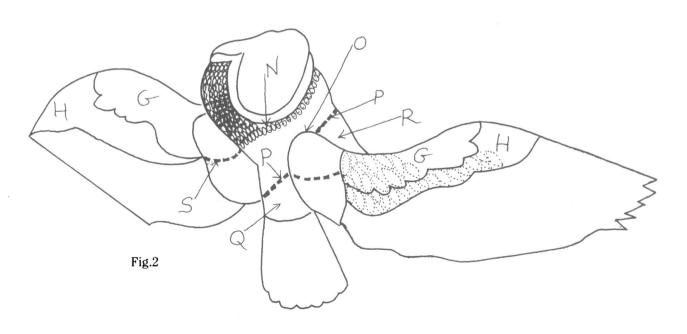

Fig.2

Now change the colour of the threads in your needle to two strands of Blanc neige mixed with one strand of 414 and fill in the section marked Q on the illustration.

Change colour again, to three strands of Blanc neige and fill in the section marked R. This sounds awfully complicated, but just keep on with your Semi-Detached Buttonholing, starting the new colour at the beginning of a row and working into the previous (different coloured) row, just as before. (You can do this for individual leaves or feathers, too, changing colours for each row if you want to).

Now do the fat shoulder sections the same way.

Start at the foundation line K (Fig.1). Use two strands of 3047 mixed with one strand of 680 until you get to the heavy dotted line (at S on the Fig.2 illustration), then change to two strands of Blanc neige mixed with one strand of 3047).

Work the other shoulder in the same way and the same colour schemes, starting at M (Fig.1) and changing colours at the heavy dotted line.

Fig.3 Fill in sections G and H making little individual feathers of Semi-Detached Buttonhole, as represented by the dotted outlines on the right-hand wing. Fill up the whole of each section, laying the feathers close together, making some small, some large, some overlapping. You can make some with, say, just a single row of buttonholing for each side of the shape, or with two rows on each side. More than that and I think you would find the feathers too bulky.

Use two strands of 435 mixed with one strand of 3047 for the G sections.

Use three strands of 3047 for the H sections.

I love the look and texture that this stitch gives.

Fig.3

Finish off the owl's body by scattering a sprinkling of Chinese Knots on top of the Semi-Detached Buttonholing. Use one strand of 310. Have a look at the photograph to see the sort of speckly effect you want (page 92).

SORBELLO STITCH

I love this stitch. (I always think of it as Saul Bellow stitch, because I love his books even more).

I have only used it for the January border, but as with other stitches in this book, you are welcome to use it for other borders if you want to chop and change a bit.

It has nothing to do with Saul Bellow, surprisingly enough, but in fact originated in the village of Sorbello in Italy where, traditionally, it was worked in heavy, white thread on a linen background. I think it works perfectly well in a lighter weight of thread and makes a pretty, lacy border.

Fig.1 Bring the needle through to the front at A and insert it at B to form a small, horizontal foundation stitch. Come through to the front again at C.

Now make a loop around the foundation stitch, just as illustrated, being careful not to pick up any of the ground fabric. (You'll probably loop it around the wrong way to start off with, if you are as daft as I was when I first tackled this stitch; I couldn't understand why I wasn't making a nice little loop until it dawned on me that I'd gone under and over the foundation stitch, instead of over and THEN under. Just look carefully at the illustration and all will be revealed.)

Fig.1
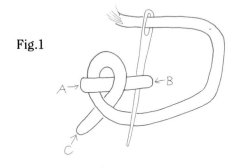

Fig.2 Complete the second loop, just as illustrated, again being careful not to pick up any of the ground fabric, and insert the needle at D. Come through to the front again at B and insert the needle at E, to make your second foundation stitch. And so on. Each stitch should be worked quite loosely and cover a tiny square area.

Fig.2 Now bring the needle through to the front again, splitting your first stitch in the middle, at C.

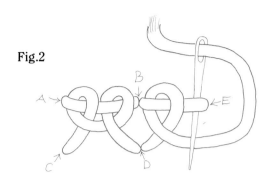

Fig.2

Fig.2

Fig.3 Pull the thread through and insert the needle again at D, to form the second stitch.

Fig.3 You can fill whole shapes with this stitch, if you want to, as illustrated, although I've just used it as a single line border in this book.

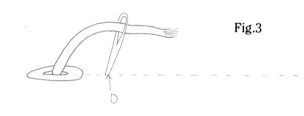

Fig.3

Fig.4 And so on, along the line. Very easy.

Fig.3

Fig.4

SPLIT STITCH

This stitch (which is also known as Kensington Outline stitch) is useful for making narrow lines. It is worked in a similar way to Stem stitch, but in this case you split each stitch as you go along.

Fig.1 Bring the needle through to the front of the fabric at A and insert at B, to form your first stitch.

STEM STITCH

Good old, useful Stem stitch. I've used it all over the place throughout this book. It's easy and quick to work and makes marvellous outlines. In fact, if you work it keeping the thread to the left of your needle as you go along, instead of to the right, it is called Outline stitch. You may find that this is the best way, for example, if you are outlining a curve where the stitches would lie best if kept to the left of the needle.

And it makes a beautiful filling stitch, too, if you work it in rows to fill a shape.

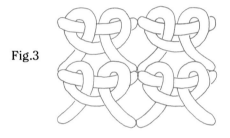

Fig.1

Fig.1   Bring the needle through to the front of the fabric at A. Insert the needle at B and come through to the front again at C, keeping the thread to the right of the needle (or to the left for Outline stitch).

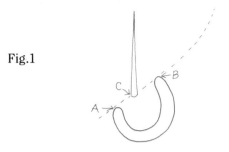

Fig.1

Fig.2   Insert the needle at D and emerge again at B, again keeping the thread to the right of the needle.

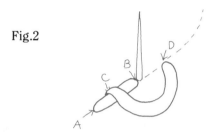

Fig.2

Fig.3   And so on, along the line, working evenly and making equal-sized stitches.

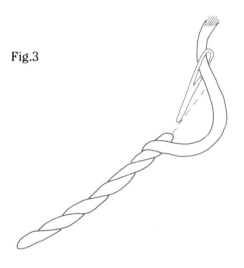

Fig.3

STRIPED WOVEN BAND

I've used this stitch in the June picture, for the border and for the wrens' wings and tails. It's another of those that look horrendously difficult on paper but actually aren't all that awful to master. You can get away with sneaky, cheating little extra stitches to fill a tiny gap and no-one will notice.

Fig.1   Lay foundation stitches, as illustrated, from 1 to 5. Now thread two blunt-ended tapestry needles, one with one colour, the other with a contrasting colour. Bring them both to the front at A, just above foundation stitch 1.

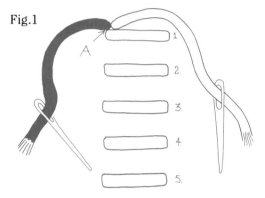

Fig.1

Fig.2   Take the dark thread and pass it UNDER foundation stitch number 1, taking care not to pick up any ground fabric. Leave this dark thread lying on the fabric, to the left, as illustrated.

Now take the light thread OVER foundation stitch number 1, and UNDER foundation stitch number 2, again taking care not to pick up any of the ground fabric. Leave the needle and thread lying on the fabric to the left, next to the dark needle and thread.

Fig.2

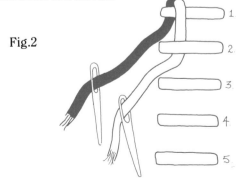

Fig.3 Pick up the dark thread again. Take it OVER the light thread lying on the fabric, OVER foundation stitch number 2 and UNDER foundation stitch number 3, as illustrated, and then lie it on the fabric to the left, just as before.

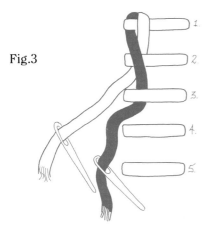

Fig.3

Fig.4 Now pick up the light thread again, take it OVER the dark thread lying on the fabric, OVER foundation stitch number 3 and UNDER foundation stitch number 4, as illustrated.

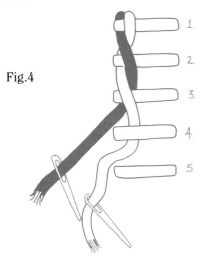

Fig.4

And so on, until you reach the last foundation stitch, then take both threads through to the back of the fabric to finish off. Start back at the top again, exactly as before.

Make sure that the dark thread always goes over the EVEN numbered foundation stitches and under the ODD numbered foundation stitches, and that the light thread does the opposite. If you alternate each row, you will get a diagonal woven band which is a variation on the theme. Birds' wings (Fig.5) are a bit trickier to work than a straight line, but as I've said, you can cheat a bit if you find yourself with any tiny gaps and no-one will notice.

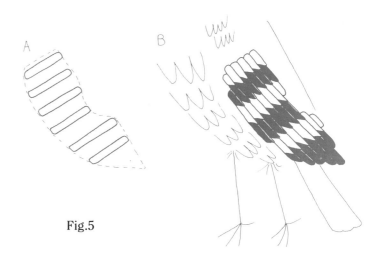

Fig.5

TURKEY WORK

This is a wonderful stitch for all the fluffy things like bumble-bees and chicks and squirrels' tails. It's very easy to work, once you have got the hang of it, and I love the fact that, just for once, you don't have to start and finish off securely. And it looks brilliantly neat on the back, which is more than can be said for most of my embroidery! That's the good news. The bad news is that it takes ages, but maybe I'm just a slow Turkey worker.

Fig.1 Don't make a knot at the end of your thread.
Take the needle through from the front of the fabric to the back at A, leaving about a quarter of an inch (½–1 cm) of thread sticking up.

Bring the needle through to the front again at B and insert again at C.

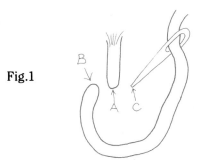

Fig.1

Fig.2   Keep the loop thus formed BELOW the line that you are working along, and don't pull this loop tight until you have brought the needle through to the front again at A.

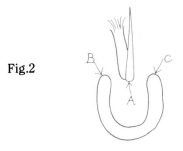

Fig.2

Fig.3   Insert the needle at D, this time keeping the thread ABOVE the line. Pull the thread through carefully, leaving a loop above the line.

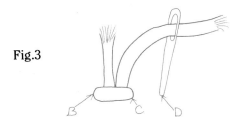

Fig.3

Fig.4   Bring the needle through to the front again at C, taking care not to draw the thread through completely, but leaving the loop above the line.

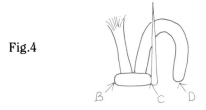

Fig.4

Fig.5   Insert the needle at E, keeping the thread BELOW the line and then emerge again at D and pull this loop tight (as in Fig.1) and so on . . .

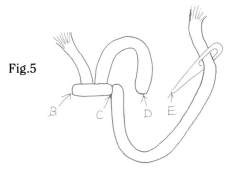

Fig.5

Fig.6   So, you alternate a loose loop stitch with a tight anchoring stitch. When you reach the end of a line, simply snip the thread off, leaving a quarter of an inch (½–1 cm) or so sticking up, just as at the beginning of the line.

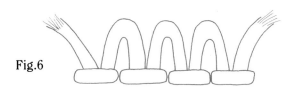

Fig.6

Fig.7   Work individual lines to fill the shape and when you've finished, cut all the loops and trim the whole shape. Don't be tempted to cut the loops until you've finished filling in the whole shape because the cut ends are much more fiddly to keep out of the way of your needle as you continue to work. You can fix the loops out of your way if they are driving you mad, by holding them flat with a long darning needle carefully pinning them to the fabric. Don't trim the shape too short until you have finished the whole picture; you will find that your hand will squash and

38

generally mess up the Turkey work and it's a good idea to have a bit of leeway so that you can re-trim any bedraggled ends once all the work is done.

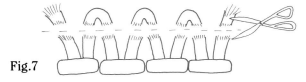

Fig.7

A different effect can be achieved by leaving the loops untrimmed, in which case you must be careful to make uniform sized loops in the first place.

PADDING WITH FELT AND BUMP

I've used a lot of padding in these pictures, to give the birds and animals, and the occasional fish and pine-cone, a marvellously fat, rounded look. It really isn't all that difficult to achieve.

'Bump' is the technical name for the soft cotton thread used for padding. I've found that DMC's Soft Cotton is the best for the purpose, but you can use more or less anything that is of a similar thickness and softness.

It helps to use roughly the same shade as the thread with which you will eventually be covering it; if you were to use dark grey bump under, say, pale pink stranded cotton, you would find it that much harder a job to cover every tiny speck. That said, you really only need to have one light and one dark shade in stock. I used a pale beige or a dark grey to cover all eventualities.

Felt is felt. You can buy squares eight and a half inches by eight and a half inches (22 x 22 cm) of it in haberdashery departments of stores like John Lewis. Again, have a light and a dark supply to cover . . . or rather, to underlay . . . all eventualities.

Use bump on its own to pad small, tricky shapes. You will need a large Milward Chenille needle. I used a No.20. These are short, sharp needles with eyes big enough for the fat bump to pass through.

I've used the Squirrel from the June picture as a good example of the various problems you will come across.

Firstly, have a good look at the Key Diagram (page 80) and the colour photograph for June (page 76). You will want the body to be good and fat and to have lovely, rounded contours at the haunch and neck.

Fig.1 Pad all the small, fiddly sections, using bump on its own. Start with small bump stitches, as illustrated by the fat, blue lines.

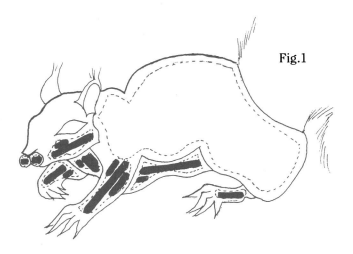

Fig.1

Fig.2 Now work over this first layer with another layer of bump, this time working in the other direction and packing the stitches closely together, as illustrated by the unshaded stitches in the diagram. You need not be fantastically accurate, just fill the area to be padded more or less neatly. You won't need another layer on the tiny little sections either side of the squirrel's mouth.

These two layers should be enough for such small areas. You can always make a particular section fatter by adding another layer of bump, but be sure to finish with a layer of stitches going against the lie of your eventual covering stitches, otherwise these covering stitches won't rest

Fig.2

smoothly on top of the padding, but will sink down between the bump stitches. That may sound terribly confusing but I think you will see what I mean if you make this particular mistake.

Now for the main bulk of the squirrel's body:

Fig.3   Cut out little pieces of felt, as indicated by the dotted line shapes in the illustration. You will need to build up layers. Start by lying the smallest onto the fabric. You can keep it in place with a single tacking stitch if you want to; I never bothered and got furious when all the little bits fell off, but if you're careful they won't, even if they are untacked. Build up the squirrel's body, adding extra layers to make the haunch chubbier, and to give a bit of a contour at the neck.

End with a layer of felt large enough to cover the whole area and keep all the little building layers in place. It does help, at this stage, to use a couple of big tacking stitches to keep the whole lot in place.

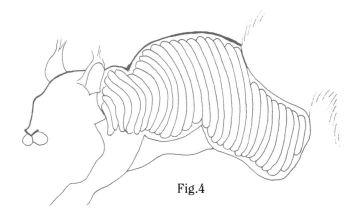

Fig.4

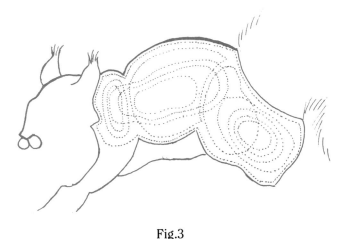

Fig.3

Fig.4   Your squirrel is now probably looking like a horrible, lumpy blob. Do not panic!

Cover the whole felt-padded area with neat rows of bump, laying the stitches close together and working them at right angles to the eventual lie of your covering stranded cotton stitches.

Now you can cover the whole squirrel as described in the specific instructions, using Roumanian Couching (page 29). Cover each section separately or running the stitches right across where it is appropriate, such as where the near foreleg joins the body.

You will find that, with practice, this is a really quite painless process. The Roumanian Couching covers large areas relatively quickly. There are occasions where I've asked you to cover padded areas with different stitches, such as Chinese Knots (page 22). Do just that. It's trickyish stopping the Chinese Knots from slipping down between the bump stitches, but pretty obvious that they will be less likely to do so if the bump is closely packed and the Knots straddle or sit on top of individual strands of the bump. I have every confidence that common sense will see you through!

USING METAL THREAD

This is a huge and complicated subject and I am only going to tackle the most rudimentary basics for the purpose of this book. I've used very little metal thread, but it helps to know roughly the best way of tackling the problems entailed. There are good books on the subject if you want to know more. The one I found most helpful was Barbara Dawson's *The Technique of Metal Thread Embroidery* which is published in paperback by Batsford.

But for the pictures in this book, all you will need to know is the following:

The basic difference between using metal threads and using ordinary sewing thread is that you don't very often take metal threads through the material but couch it on the surface. This is because the metal thread would weaken the fabric and itself and is, in any case, too expensive to want to waste it where it can't be seen. I've cheated with the Silver Divisible on bits like the January icicles, and used ordinary Stem stitch (page 35), but that was just laziness and didn't actually make my life any easier.

This is what you should do:
First pad the area if the specific instructions ask for it, such as for the Kingfisher's head in the September picture.

The Elizabeth Stuart Cord is 3-stranded and I have used all three strands at all times.

The DMC Silver Divisible is also 3-stranded and sometimes I have asked you to separate it and use just a single strand. Not an easy task!

Fig.1   Lay the metal thread on the surface to be covered, leaving about an inch (2–3 cm) free. Now couch the metal thread with tiny stitches (shaded blue in the illustration) lying at right angles to it, in a single strand of cotton which will be as invisible as possible. Space these little couching stitches about every quarter of an inch (½–1 cm) along the line and making the last couching stitch about a quarter of an inch (½–1 cm) from the end of the line. Pull the metal thread very gently as you work the row to keep it straight. Work the couching stitches firmly so that they won't shift about when the fabric is eventually removed from the embroidery ring. Leave about an inch (2–3 cm) of the metal thread free at the end.

Continue working row after row like this until you have filled in the area, leaving all the free ends to be taken through to the back when you have finished. If you take

them through to the back as you go along, they can get into the most awful tangle underneath.

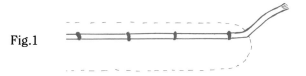

Fig.1

Fig.2   Use a No.18 Chenille needle and insert it into the fabric right up to the eye, where the metal thread is to be taken through to the back, at A on the illustration.

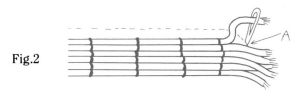

Fig.2

Now thread your little tail end of metal thread into the eye of the needle and pull it through to the back. Do all the little beginning and ending tails in the same way. It's the most ghastly, fiddlesome job, but there aren't vast areas to be worked in this way, so be patient!
You don't need to sew the ends in place on the underside. You can catch them out of the way over work already completed, with a few tacking stitches if it helps, of if they are not in your way just leave them.

BLUE TITS · *Parus caerulus*
RABBIT · *Oryctolagus cuniculus*
WESTERN HEMLOCK · *Tsuga heterophylla*

January

It is quite an alarming prospect, starting out on the first of twelve embroideries, knowing you have to finish the whole lot in a short time and write all the instructions and do all the key diagrams and sound as if you know what you're talking about! The good thing about doing every stitch yourself is that you *do* know what you are talking about, even if you are not necessarily doing it as brilliantly as someone with masses of experience. It is an advantage in a way, to be less knowledgeable; I think the cleverer you become, the more you forget what it is like to be a beginner and the more you take it for granted that you will be understood.

So, if you are tremendously experienced, you will probably make a better job of these blue tits than I did, and if you are a beginner, as I was, you can see from the photograph that you can make a perfectly lovely embroidery and not feel that you dare not tackle something which looks difficult.

It wasn't until I started thinking about the first picture that I even considered using padding to make the birds and animals have some sort of dimension. I'd never used this technique before and wasn't even sure that it existed, so ignorant was I. I just knew that I needed to breathe life into the pictures. In order to see if the padding idea would work, I began the 'Anna' sampler which you can see in the Introduction to this book. I cut out bits of felt and used soft cotton and managed a rough version of what has come to be the most important feature of these embroideries. I'd never heard of 'bump'. I later learned from the Royal School of Needlework, once I'd got up enough courage to cross their threshold and discovered how helpful and kind they were, that this is the proper name for the sort of soft cotton you use for padding. I learnt more, too, about 'stump work' which is roughly what I'm doing, where things like coats of arms are padded to give a raised effect. Thrilling. A whole new way to make a picture come to life.

Believe it or not, there are two blue tits outside my window at this very moment. I do love these funny, energetic little birds. I live in the middle of London and am lucky enough to have a balcony outside huge French windows. The blue tits come to feed off coconut halves that I hang up for them, and they are a constant source of pleasure, and as it turns out, inspiration for this embroidery.

You might, if you happen to have a pet rabbit, like to change my rabbit's colour scheme to look like yours. It's quite fun to add personal things like that. Don't forget to buy the appropriate coloured stranded cotton if you do.

COLOURS YOU WILL NEED

(DMC Stranded Cotton, 1 skein of each unless otherwise stated)
No. 455 (pale yellow)
No. 444 (darker yellow)
No. 3053 (pale olive green)
No. 503 (pale green)
No. 501 (dark green)
No. 932 (pale blue)
No. 930 (dark blue)
No. 793 (lilac)
No. 801 (dark brown)
No. 680 (golden brown)
No. 612 (light brown) 2 skeins
No. 310 (black)
Blanc neige (white) 2 skeins
1 spool of Silver Divisible (DMC ref. no: D283)
Bump and Felt for padding

STITCHES YOU WILL NEED TO KNOW

Stem (p.35)
Satin (p.29)
Satin Stitch Couching (p.30)
Raised Fishbone (p.27)
Detached Overcast (p.23)
Roumanian Couching (p.29)
Portuguese Knotted Stem (p.26)
Sorbello (p.34)
Chinese Knots (p.22)
Turkey Work (p.37)

GENERAL NOTES

Trace the Detailed Outline and transfer onto your fabric as described in the chapter on General Know-How (p.17).
Use the colour photograph and the Key Diagram to help you follow the instructions.

The shaded areas on the Key Diagram represent all the padded sections. Don't try and fill in all the padding first, do each section as you come to it in the instructions. You will find it much easier, for example, to fill in the unpadded bits of the birds' faces before you pad the tops of the heads and cheeks. Read the instructions for Padding with Felt and Bump (p.39).

Read the instructions for any stitches with which you are unfamiliar. Do use the right size and type of needle. It really does make a difference. See the chapter on General Know-How (p.17).

INSTRUCTIONS

Blue tits

Outline the beaks of each bird, using one strand of 310 in tiny Stem stitch.

Fill in the black parts of each birds' face, using two strands of 310 in Satin stitch.
Now pad the sections of each bird indicated by the shaded areas in the Key Diagram. Pad the breasts quite fatly and ignore where the legs go across the padded section; the legs will be added on top of the breasts later. Cover the white parts of the face using two strands of Blanc neige in Satin stitch.

Fill in each beak, using one strand of Blanc neige in tiny Satin stitch.

Make the white highlight in the centre of each eye with a single Chinese Knot for each using two strands of Blanc neige.

Cover the crown of each head using two strands of 793 mixed with one strand of 932 in Satin stitch.

Cover the padding of the breasts using two strands of 445 mixed with one strand of 444 in Roumanian Couching.

Now do the wings. Outline all the little wing feathers using one strand of 310 in tiny Stem stitch.

Fill in the shoulder feathers, shaded in dots on the Key Diagram, using two strands of 3053 in Raised Fishbone stitch.

Fill in the blue feathers using two strands of 930 mixed with one strand of 932, again in Raised Fishbone stitch.

Now do the tails of two of the birds, leaving the tail of the top bird until you have completed the borders. Use two strands of 310 in Stem stitch lines, alternating with Stem stitch lines of two strands of 930 mixed with one strand of 932.

Leave the legs and feet until later.

Western Hemlock

The trunk and branches of the tree and all of the first border (see Key Diagram) are done in Portuguese Knotted Stem stitch using three strands of 612. I've made two knots around each stitch (see stitch instructions) for a knobbly effect. It's a rather slow stitch to work but worth the effort. For the leaves, use three strands of 503. Each spikey little leaf is made by first laying a long stitch the length of the leaf and then covering this foundation stitch with tiny slanting Satin stitch and then outlining with one strand of 501 in tiny Stem stitch. Where the leaves overlap each other, work the underneath leaf first and then work

DETAILED OUTLINE

KEY DIAGRAM

the overlapping one on top of it. Those leaves which overlap the border will have to be left till later.

Now do the cones. Pad each tiny little section as shown by the shaded areas on the Key Diagram. You will need only one or two stitches of bump for each little pad. Now cover each of these little sections using three strands of 612 in Satin stitch and outline each one using one strand of 801 in tiny Stem stitch.

Rabbit

Pad the sections indicated by the shaded areas on the Key Diagram.

Do the pupil of the eye using two strands 310 in Stem stitch. Outline the eye using two strands of Blanc neige in Stem stitch. Do the brown 'eyebrow' using two strands of 801.

Do the highlight of the eye using two strands of Blanc neige and making a single Chinese Knot.

Do the nose using two strands of 310 in a couple of tiny straight stitches. Do the rabbit's right ear using two strands of 801 in Stem stitch and add a few random stitches of 612 on top of the brown foundation. Do the rabbit's left ear (not the sticky-up one!) using one strand of Blanc neige for the white line, in Stem stitch, filled in with two strands of 680 in Stem stitch. Outline the white line with a line of one strand of 801 mixed with one strand of 612 in Stem stitch and do the outside edge of the ear in three strands of 680 in Satin stitch. Do the white 'ruff' at the neck, using three strands of Blanc neige in straight stitches to form a spikey line (have a look at the photograph since you will have covered the drawing by now with padding). Now do the rest of the body, covering the padding in rough straight stitches to give a shaggy effect. Use combinations of 801, 612 and 680. Mix two strands of 680, say, with one of 612, or use three strands of any one colour. Use 801 for the shadier bits, like around the white ruff and along the line of the haunch.

Add the whisker 'dots' (well, what are they really called?) using one strand of 310 in a Chinese Knot for each dot. Do the whiskers, again using one strand of 310, in Stem stitch.

You will have to leave the paw that overlaps the border till later.

Do the tail using two strands of Blanc neige in Turkey Work. Don't trim the tail too short until you have finished the whole picture; you can always trim some more then, if you have left yourself enough to play with. If you cut it too short it may get rather bedraggled and you won't be able to tidy it up later.

Snow

Pad all the snowy bits as indicated by the shaded sections on the Key Diagram. Now you have the merry task of covering all this padding with hundreds of maddening, hysteria-inducing beastly little Chinese Knots using three strands of Blanc neige. Good luck. If you get as bad-tempered about it as I did, finish off a border or two in between Chinese Knotting. It might help. Outline the snow sections in two strands of the Silver Divisible in Stem stitch. This is another thrill guaranteed to have you tearing your hair out . . . it is a perfect nightmare trying to separate up the silver. And a fairly good nightmare trying to do Stem stitch with same, but that is because you shouldn't really use metal thread in this way. I just felt that, since there is so little, maybe I could get away with it. (See Metal Thread instructions, p.40, for the proper method.)

Icicles

More of the dreaded Silver Divisible, but at least I haven't asked you to divide it this time; use all three strands and lay a long stitch the length of the icicle and cover it with little slanting Satin stitches, just as you did for each of the spikey leaves of the tree.

Borders

First: you have already done this as part of the Western Hemlock branches.
Second: use Satin Stitch Couching. Pad with four strands of bump (see stitch instructions) and cover with three strands of 501.
Third: three strands of 801 in Stem stitch.
Fourth: three strands of 930 in Sorbello stitch.
Fifth: Satin Stitch Couching, again using four strands of bump for the padding, covered with three strands of Blanc neige.
Sixth: six strands of 801 in Stem stitch.
Last: Straight Satin stitch, using two strands of 932 for the top and bottom borders and two strands of 793 for the left and right sides.

Now you can finish off all the overlapping bits: the top bird's tail, the bits of tree and the rabbit's paw.

For the birds' legs and feet, use one strand of 310 mixed with one strand of 612. Work ordinary Overcast for the legs and Detached Overcast for the feet that curl around the branch or over the border.

And don't forget to trim the rabbit's tail!

PIED WAGTAILS · *Motacilla alba yarrelli*
GARDEN SNAIL · *Helix aspersa*
WINTER ACONITE · *Eranthis hyemalis*
IVY · *Hedera helix*

February

I'd never seen pied wagtails, city dweller that I am, until one day I drove up to Sandy in Bedfordshire for a meeting at the Royal Society for the Protection of Birds and there were all these wagtails tail-wagging in the RSPB carpark. They must have known that even the carpark was safe, if it had anything to do with that organization. Anyway, there they were and they reminded me of a story I'd read somewhere of a pair of wagtails nesting on the mudguard of a car belonging to a teacher at a school on the Isle of Man. The birds simply waited for the car to arrive each day so that they could carry on with their nest building! I don't know what they thought was going on at weekends, or how the chicks fared once they'd hatched, zooming around the Isle of Man, or even whether the whole story is made up, but it's a nice thought. I went in to my meeting full of enthusiasm for pied wagtails and here they are, glorifying an RSPB calendar and this book.

Don't be put off by all those feathers. They are quite a lot easier to embroider than they were to draw, so take heart. The whole picture is relatively uncomplicated. The ivy leaves are gorgeously simple and so are the winter aconites. I got into a bit of a muddle with the snail's shell, all that coiled padding seemed to be tricky to handle, but you can thin it out by chopping off a few strands of the bump as you get into the tighter coils of the shell's centre.

The ivy stems curling around the borders and fence seem to fascinate people; Detached Overcast is not my most favourite stitch, but the effect is terrific, so I don't mind putting up with it. You may have more patience than I had and find my antipathy to this inoffensive and not very difficult stitch to be incomprehensible. I just find it maddeningly fiddly and tiresome.

I've used fairly simple ideas for the borders. You don't have to stick to my suggestions if you have other exciting line stitches in your repertoire and would like to use them. See how you go; if you are as inexperienced as I was when I did this embroidery, you might prefer to stay safely with my undemanding methods but if you are feeling brave, use these borders for experimenting. Follow my colour scheme roughly and don't forget that different stitches use up different quantities of thread, so that if you use your own ideas, you may need more or less than I have allowed for.

COLOURS YOU WILL NEED

(DMC Stranded Cotton, 1 skein of each unless otherwise stated)
No. 3047 (cream)
No. 3032 (beige)
No. 729 (yellowy ochre)
No. 500 (dark green)
No. 3053 (pale olive green)
No. 414 (lightish grey)
No. 413 (dark grey)
No. 444 (cadmium yellow)
No. 445 (lemon yellow) 2 skeins
No. 310 (black)
Blanc neige (white)
Bump for padding

STITCHES YOU WILL NEED TO KNOW

Stem (p.35)
Satin (p.29)
Satin Stitch Couching (p.30)
Split (p.35)
Roumanian Couching (p.29)
Overcast (p.25)
Detached Overcast (p.23)
Chinese Knot (p.22)

GENERAL NOTES

Trace the Detailed Outline and transfer onto your fabric as described in the chapter on General Know-How (p.17). It will help you if you draw the ivy stalks as faintly as possible so that your Detached Overcasting won't show horrible pen lines underneath. Quite a lot of stalk and several of the leaves will be laid over other, border stitches anyway so you will be using the photograph and detailed outline for guidance. It sounds tricky, but really isn't. It couldn't matter less if your stalks don't follow exactly the same route as mine.

The same applies to the ivy leaves: don't bother to draw in all the little veins, since they will have to be added after you have done the dark green of the leaf itself. They do not need exactly to follow the drawing but can be added more or less as I have shown without panicking about being the very same.

Use the colour photograph and the Key Diagram to help you to follow the instructions.

The shaded areas on the Key Diagram represent the padded sections of the birds and the snail's shell. Pad each section as you come to it in the instructions, using the specific instructions for Padding with Felt and Bump to help you (p.39).

Do use the right size and type of needle. It really does make a difference. See the chapter on General Know-How (p.17).

INSTRUCTIONS

Winter Aconites

Flowers: use three strands of 444 in Stem stitch for the darker yellow petals, shaded with dots on the Key Diagram. Use three strands of 445, again in Stem stitch for the pale yellow petals. Use three strands of 3053 in Stem stitch for the grey centre of the bigger flower. Use two strands of 500 in tiny, slanting Stem stitch for the dark green leaves under each flower.

Stems: use two strands of bump per stem to pad them out and cover with Satin Stitch Couching using three strands of 3047. Start at the flower end of each stem and when you get to the border, cut off any extra bump. The join where the bottom of the stem meets the border will be finished off when you do the border.

Borders

I did all the borders next, since so much of the rest of the picture overlaps them.
First: use four strands of bump (see instructions for Satin Stitch Couching) and cover with three strands of 3047. When you get to where the aconite stems meet the border, use longer stitches to incorporate the stem and make it look as if it is growing out of the border.
Second: use one strand of 310 in Stem stitch.
Third: three strands of 444 in Stem stitch
Fourth: three strands of 3053 in Stem stitch.
Fifth: three strands of 445 in Stem stitch.
Sixth: three strands of 729 in Stem stitch.
Seventh: three strands of 445 in Stem stitch.
Eighth: three strands of 3053 in Stem stitch.
Ninth: three strands of 444 in Stem stitch.
Tenth: now do another border of Satin Stitch Couching, using four strands of bump for the padding, covered with three strands of 414.
Eleventh: finish with a border of straight Satin stitch using two strands of 445. You can make the edge look

DETAILED OUTLINE

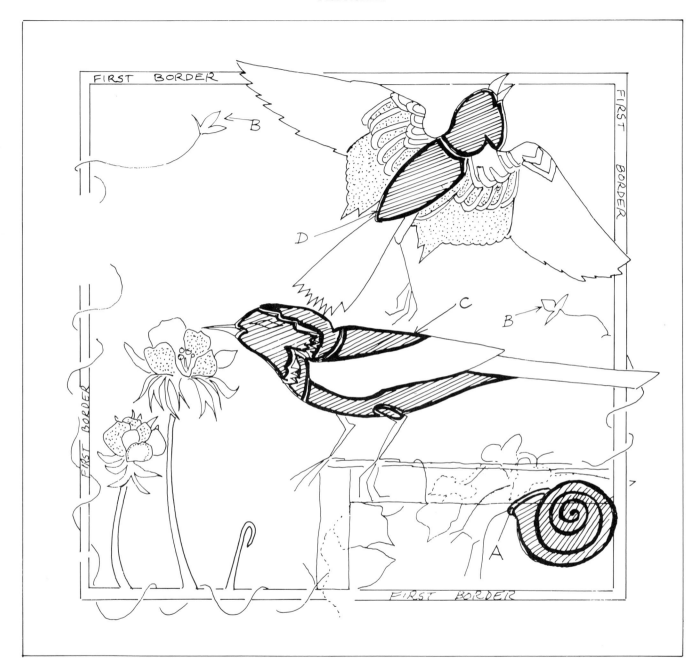

KEY DIAGRAM

neater if you outline it first with a foundation line of split or stem stitch. It's rather a boring chore, since the stitches will be covered by the Satin stitch, but does make a tidier finish.

Fence

Do the top edge of the fence in slanting Satin stitch, using three strands of 3032. Now fill in the rest of the fence, again using three strands of 3032, in vertical Stem stitch lines for the upright bit and horizontal lines for the cross bar. Fill in the whole fence, going straight over where the leaves and snail will eventually be. These will be added on top of the fence stitching.

Snail

Do the 'lip' of the shell (A on the Key Diagram), padding it with a strand of bump and covering with three strands of 729 in Satin Stitch Couching. Next, cut five strands of bump, each long enough to complete the whole spiral of the shell. Starting at the lip of the shell, cover the bump with three strands of 729 in Satin Stitch Couching, working your way in a spiral to the centre. You can always cut off a strand or two of the bump as you get to the tighter centre if you feel that the padding is getting too fat and clumsy.

Now add the stripes on top of the Satin Stitch Couching, using three strands of 414 in a 'V' shape.

Do the body in Chinese Knots. Make some of the knots in two strands of 3053 and some in two strands of 3047.

Do the stalks of the eyes using two strands of 3047 in tiny slanting Satin stitch and put a Chinese Knot on top of each of the two longer stalks, using one strand of 310 mixed with one strand of 3047.

Ivy

For the leaves, use three strands of 500 in slanting Satin stitch. The little leaves at the tip of the stalks (B on the Key Diagram) are in three strands of 3053. Where the leaves cross over the borders, do just that, laying the stitches carefully on top of the border stitches. Add the veins, using one strand of 3053 in Split stitch. As I've said in the General Notes, it really doesn't matter how accurate the veins are, just follow the photograph or detailed diagram for guidance or make them up as you go along.

Do the brown stem in 3032, using six strands for the foundation and working Overcast and Detached Overcast in two strands over it. You will need to use Detached Overcast wherever the stem crosses over the border or the

fence and you will find it much easier if you change your sharp needle to a blunt-ended tapestry needle.

Pied Wagtails

Pad all the sections represented by the shaded areas on the Key Diagram.

Foreground bird: cover the padded areas in Roumanian Couching, using three strands of Blanc neige for the white face and breast, three strands of 310 for the black stripe and top of the head and two strands of 413 mixed with one strand of 310 for the back (C on the Key Diagram).

Do the eye using one strand of 310 in tiny Split stitch, leaving a speck of the white showing for the highlight. Outline the beak, again in one strand of 310 in tiny Stem stitch. Fill in the beak using one strand of 413 in tiny Satin stitch.

Do the black part of the tail using three strands of 310 in rows of Stem stitch. Do the white line along the tail using three strands of Blanc neige in small, slanting Satin stitch. Do the grey line in three strands of 413 in Stem stitch. Where the tail overlaps the border, just lay the stitches straight on top of the border stitches.

Outline each wing feather using three strands of Blanc neige in Overcast stitch, then fill in each feather using two strands of 413 in slanting Satin stitch.

Do the little white tops to the legs using two strands of Blanc neige in stem stitch. Do the legs and feet using two strands of 413 in Overcast stitch.

Now, outline all of the white part of the head, the breast and the tops of the legs in one strand of 310 in tiny Stem stitch.

Flying bird: Cover the padded areas in Roumanian Couching, using three strands of Blanc neige for the white face, three strands of 310 for the black bits and three strands of 413 for the back (D on the Key Diagram). Outline the beak using one strand of 310 in tiny Stem stitch, taking the stitches across the border where the beak does so. Fill in with one strand of 413 in tiny Satin stitch.

Do the leg and foot using one strand of 413 in Stem stitch. Do the white top of the leg in two strands of Blanc neige in Stem stitch outlined with one strand of 413 in Stem stitch.

Now do the wings; use the photograph and Key Diagram to guide you. Outline the white edged feathers using two strands of Blanc neige in Overcast stitch. Outline all the other feathers in two strands of 310 for the larger, primary feathers and one strand for the smaller ones, all in Stem stitch. Now fill in the feathers. All the feathers represented by the dotted areas on the Key Diagram should be filled with one strand of 414 in tiny Stem stitch rows. All the remaining feathers should be filled in using two strands of 413, again in Stem stitch rows.

For the tail, use two strands of 310 in rows of Stem stitch for the central, black panel. Use two strands of Blanc neige for the white bits. Add the bird's eye, making a Chinese Knot of one strand of 310 mixed with two strands of 413.

March

In the early stages of work on these designs, I had one of many meetings at the Royal Society for the Protection of Birds, à propos the calendar for 1990 from which the book originated. This particular meeting was about what birds should be included. Jeremy Hawtrey-Woore who is the General Manager of sales at the RSPB and has, amongst other far more important things, to deal with people like me who come to see him with mad ideas about embroidered calendars, was going through popular and not so popular birds (well, you wouldn't really want a crow or a vulture to embroider, would you?) and said that lots of people loved the Diver. I think he expected me to say did he mean Greg Luganis, but instead I thought I'd show off a bit and said, did he mean *Gavia arctica* or *Gavia stellata*? I didn't want him to think that I was just any old non-ornithologically minded actress, which I'm sure is exactly what he did think! Well, that went down awfully well, I can tell you! I can't remember why I knew the Latin names for divers, but it sounded good and thank heavens I got it right. I love the Latin names, which is why I've included them with each picture, not because I imagine the world to be seething with zoological, botanical and ornithological embroiderers, nor to be idiotically pretentious, but just because they are so interesting.

Anyway, I think I improved the impression I was trying so hard to make on Jeremy, knowing that the Diver he meant, which turned out to be the Black Throated one, was called Gavia arctica.

In America, this bird is called an Arctic Loon, which is much nicer. I don't know why we can't all call them loons. I do . . . when I'm not showing off the fact that I know two words of Latin.

They obviously are popular birds. This embroidery has been one of the most admired in the whole book, funnily enough. I think the size and fatness of the bird, and the simplicity of the overall design seem to be attractive. It's not terribly hard to do. You mustn't panic that you can't draw in all the black and white feathers to guide you, since your guidelines would be covered by padding. It's not difficult to refer to the photograph and Detailed Outline as you go along and you can even mark the padding with your indelible pen, if it helps. And it couldn't matter less if a few of your bird's feathers are in a slightly different place from those of my bird. No two loons are identical, after all, as I've pointed out in the instructions.

BLACK THROATED DIVER · *Gavia arctica*
PERCH · *Perca fluviatilis*

COLOURS YOU WILL NEED

(DMC Stranded Cotton, 1 skein of each unless otherwise stated)
No. 799 (pale blue)
No. 792 (dark blue)
No. 926 (green-ish blue) 2 skeins
No. 646 (grey)
No. 413 (dark grey)
No. 451 (light grey)
No. 921 (orange)
No. 612 (beige)
No. 610 (brown)
No. 310 (black)
Blanc neige (white) 2 skeins
1 spool of Silver Divisible (DMC ref. no: D283)
Bump and Felt for padding.
You will need 1 strand of scarlet for the bird's eye; I used a bit of cotton because it seemed silly to buy a whole skein for just one tiny thread.

STITCHES YOU WILL NEED TO KNOW

Stem (p.35)
Satin (p.29)
Satin Stitch Couching (p.30)
Roumanian Couching (p.29)
Chinese Knot (p.22)
Detached Chain (p.23)

GENERAL NOTES

Trace the Detailed Outline and transfer it onto your fabric, as described in the chapter on General Know-How (p.17). Don't bother to trace more than the outline of the padded sections (see the Key Diagram to guide you) since any detail will be covered by the padding anyway.

Use the colour photograph and the Key Diagram to help you follow the instructions. The shaded areas on the Key Diagram represent all the padded sections. Tackle each section as you come to it in the instructions. Read the specific instructions for Padding with Felt and Bump to help you (p.39).

Read the instructions for any stitches with which you are unfamiliar. Do use the right size and type of needle, it really does help. See the chapter on General Know-How (p.17).

INSTRUCTIONS

Fish

Do the tail and the lower fins first; use two strands of 612 for the stripes and two strands of 921 for the orange bits, all in Stem stitch lines.

Now do the dorsal fin (the big one on the fish's back) and the adipose fin (the one nearer the tail on the fish's back and I bet you didn't know that that was what it was called . . . I didn't), using two strands of 610 for the stripes (I'm sure they're not called mere stripes, but never mind!) and two strands of 612 for the rest, all in Stem stitch.

Now pad the body of the fish. Make it quite fat, using little bits of felt, built up in layers and covered with a layer of bump. Using the Detailed Outline and the photograph to guide you, cover this padding with Detached Chain stitches, using two strands of 610 for the stripes, two strands of 612 for the beige part of the body and one strand of 612 mixed with one strand of Blanc neige for the underbelly.

Add the little pectoral fin (that's the one nearest to the gill), outlining it with one strand of 612 in Stem stitch and filling it in with Stem stitch stripes, alternating one strand of 612 with one strand of 610.

Add the fine stripe that runs the length of the body (the lateral line, if you're really interested, marked A on the Key Diagram if you're totally confused) using one strand of 413 in tiny Stem stitch. Leave the fish's head until later, when you have done the borders. I'll tell you how to do it when we get to it.

Black Throated Diver

Pad all the areas indicated by the shaded sections of the diagram except for the beak and the tips of the tail feathers which you will have to do after the borders. Use layers of felt covered with bump for the large areas and bump on its own for the little bits. Don't panic at this stage and wonder how you are going to cope with no guidelines for all the feathers. You can draw them roughly on top of the bump or simply keep looking at the Detailed Outline drawing or the photograph to guide you. You don't have to be absolutely exact or worry if your feathers aren't in precisely the same place as mine; after all, every Black Throated Diver is different!

Start with the head. Thread one needle with three strands of 413 and another needle with one strand of 413. Fill in the area indicated on the Key Diagram with a B, laying long, smooth Satin stitches with the three strands and couching them down as invisibly as you can with

DETAILED OUTLINE

slanting stitches using the single strand of the same colour. I know it sounds incredibly complicated but you will see what I mean as soon as you have done the first stitch. You could lay down all the long Satin stitches first and then fix them in place but I personally found it much easier to do each one as I went along. When you have finished the B section, fill in the C section in exactly the same way, this time using three strands of 646 held in place with one strand of the 646. Then finish covering the rest of the head the same way, but using three strands of 451, again held in place with one strand of 451.

Now do the eye, laying the stitches on top of the background colour and being a bit careful not to disturb the smoothness of the Satin stitches more than you can help. Tricky-ish. Outline the eye in tiny Satin stitches using two strands of 451. Fill in with your ordinary red cotton in tiny Stem stitch. Add the pupil with a couple of tiny straight stitches in one strand of 310 and put a single Chinese Knot, using one strand of Blanc neige, in the centre of the pupil to highlight it.

I'll explain how to do the beak later, when the borders have been completed. Leave it for now.

Neck: fill in the section indicated by a D on the Key Diagram, using three strands of 413 in Stem stitch. Fill in the section indicated by the E on the Key Diagram, using three strands of 310 in Stem stitch.

Do the stripes in three strands of 310 in Stem stitch, again not worrying if you don't match exactly what I've done. Use the photograph and the Detailed Outline to guide you and draw lines on top of the padding if it makes things easier. Fill in all the white bits of the neck and breast using three strands of Blanc neige in Stem stitch. Don't forget the under-water bits (indicated by the F on the Key Diagram).

Now for the wings. Using three strands of 310, fill in all the black stripes and zig-zags, using little straight stitches. Don't make the stripes too neat, they should be a bit bedraggled at the edges. Use the photograph and the Detailed Outline to guide you. Outline the tail feathers except for the tips that overlap the border, and all along the waterline from tail to foot, using two strands of 310 in Stem stitch. Fill in all the white bits, including the spots on the tail feathers and the tail feather stripes, using two strands of Blanc neige in Chinese Knots for the spots and Stem stitch for the stripes on the tail.

Leave the tips of the tail feathers until after you have finished the borders.

Now fill in all the grey, using three strands of 413. The sections indicated on the Key Diagram by little dots are also filled in with three strands of 413. Use little straight stitches or Stem stitch, whichever fills the space best.

Outline the fat wing section (G on the Key Diagram) using three strands of 451 in Stem stitch.

Foot: Cover the padding of the leg and 'toes', using two strands of 646 in Stem stitch for the leg and Satin stitch for the toes and the knuckley bit (I haven't done my research properly and discovered the technical terms for these esoteric portions of bird anatomy . . . I got carried away with adipose fins on the fish, I think, and lost interest when it came to bird's toes or whatever they're called). Anyway, fill in the webs (at least we all know what they are!) of the foot, using long, silky straight stitches in one strand of 451.

Water

Use the photograph to guide you as to the sequence of colours. Use three strands of 799, three strands of 792 or three strands of 926. Cross over the bird's foot and the fish's fins where indicated (quite tough getting through the padding, but not impossible) and then, between each section of colour, do a line of Stem stitch in the Silver. It's no fun, using metal thread in this rule-breaking way. I can see why they make the rules but I don't think, along with bird foot terminology, I had thoroughly investigated the technique when I decided that Stem stitch would do, and, actually, it does look good. So if you would rather learn from the specific instructions for using metal thread and do it that way, feel free. I wrote those instructions too late to benefit from them myself, such is my chaotic way of approach.

Borders

First: the water makes up the bottom line of the first border. For the other three sides, use three strands of 926 in Stem stitch.

Second: three strands of 926 in Stem stitch, again going around three sides of the square, omitting the bottom line.

Third: another border of three strands of 926 in Stem stitch, once again going around three sides of the square and omitting the bottom line.

Fourth: do a border of Satin Stitch Couching around all four sides of the frame, using four strands of bump for the padding, covered with three strands of 646.

All the subsequent borders go around all four sides of the frame.

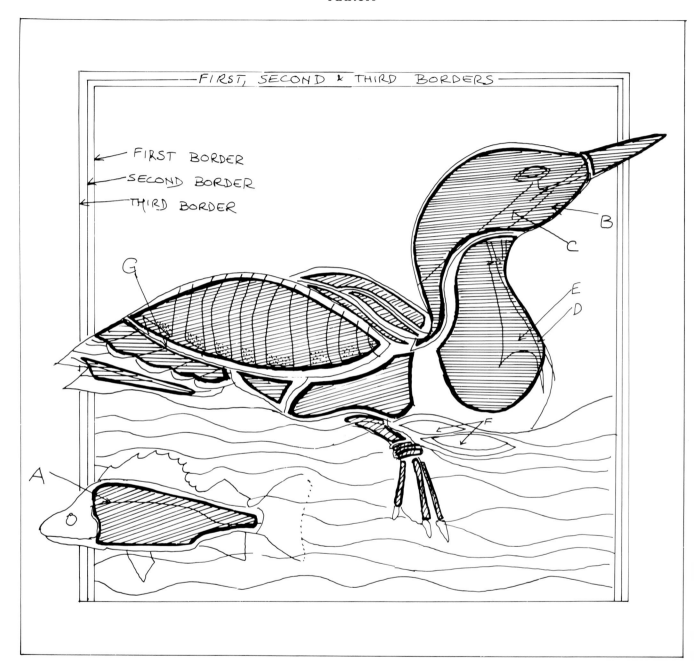

FIRST, SECOND & THIRD BORDERS

FIRST BORDER
SECOND BORDER
THIRD BORDER

B

C

E

D

G

F

A

KEY DIAGRAM

Fifth: six strands of Blanc neige in Stem stitch.

Sixth: three strands of 413 in Stem stitch.

Seventh: three strands of Blanc neige in Stem stitch.

Eighth: Satin Stitch Couching using four strands of bump for the padding, covered with three strands of 921.

Ninth: end with a frame of straight Satin stitch, using two strands of 926. You will achieve a neater edge if you first outline it with a foundation of Stem or Split stitch. It's awfully boring to go slogging all the way round with stitches that will be covered up by the Satin stitches, but does give a tidier end result. Yours will probably be tidier than mine anyway; I'm not terribly fussy about how straight a straight line should be, as I expect you will have noticed!

Now finish off the poor headless fish: outline the eye, the shape of the gill and the mouth, using one strand of 310 in tiny Stem stitch. Use the photograph to guide you and fill in the nose (do fish have noses?) with two strands of 612, outlined with two strands of 610, all in Stem or straight stitches. Use one strand of Blanc neige to outline under the mouth, in Stem stitch or one long straight stitch which will lie easily over all the border padding. Fill in the 'cheek' and below the eye with two strands of 926 in straight stitches. Fill in any other bits that I've missed telling you about in my enthusiasm for technicalities, with 612 or 610 or anything that cheers you up.

Pad the bird's beak to even it across the bumpy surface of all those borders. Outline with two strands of 310 in tiny Stem stitch, and do the line down the middle in the same way. Add the white lines using two strands of Blanc neige in long, straight stitches. Fill in the rest with two strands of 451 in long, straight stitches, held in place if necessary, by tiny couching stitches. It's quite fiddly, this beak, but take your time and if you have made the padding nice and even, it won't be so tricky.

Finish off the tail feathers, outlining with two strands of 310 in Stem stitch. Fill in the bits of white stripe, using two strands of Blanc neige in Stem stitch. Fill in the grey, using three strands of 413.

GOLDCREST · *Regulus regulus*
WHITE-TAILED BUMBLEBEE · *Bombus lucorum*
CORSICAN PINE · *Pinus nigra*

April

I think that this might be my favourite of all the embroideries. They are all so different, but this one just pleases me, I don't know why. I do love goldcrests, for a start, perhaps because they are the smallest birds we have and anyway, they are so adorable. The bit of the picture that I like the very best is the spider's web, tucked away amongst the feathers and leaves of the goldcrests' nest. It's one of those ridiculous little details that pleases me most and I don't appear to be alone; everyone who has seen this embroidery loves the spider's web, once they have spotted it.

The bumble-bee, apart from being perfect in the design, is for my dear friend Bill Gibb, to whom this book is dedicated. He used a bee as a sort of signature . . . 'B' for Billy. He was a brilliantly talented fashion designer who gave me a lot of advice and help on this embroidered calendar and book idea that I first had in 1987. He died in January 1988, but I feel that he's here in spirit, giving the encouragement he always gave so generously. So the bumble-bee is a symbol for me of someone very special and much missed.

You can really go to town on the nest. I kept it fairly simple because, from the point of view of having to photograph and show the work clearly, I didn't want to clutter it up too much and above all, didn't want completely to obscure my treasured spider's web. I'm sure you could safely add more feathery excrescences. Just imagine what a goldcrest might use for its nest and build one yourself. Easy. Easier, even, than for goldcrests, since birds can't go to John Lewis for feathers if they're hard to come by. I couldn't find any anywhere, except for a few rather mouldy ones that I filched out of an old pillow, but the haberdashery departments of big stores seem to go in for this sort of thing.

The Portuguese Knotted Stem stitch makes wonderful, knobbly branches. It's a bit on the slow side to work but worth the effort. You can always get away with ordinary Stem stitch if you are feeling frightfully lazy, but the Portuguese version isn't all that difficult to learn if it doesn't happen to be in your repertoire and I think you'll be glad if you make the effort.

COLOURS YOU WILL NEED

DMC Stranded Cotton, 1 strand of each unless otherwise stated)
No. 3031 (dark brown)
No. 731 (dark olive green)
No. 469 (brighter green)
No. 3053 (pale grey-ish green)
No. 817 (scarlet)
No. 725 (yellow)
No. 3032 (beige)
No. 3047 (cream)
No. 3045 (golden beige) 2 skeins
No. 413 (dark grey)
No. 310 (black)
Blanc neige (white)
Bump and Felt for padding.

You will need feathers and bits of wool or mohair for the nest, anything you have around that seems like good nest-making material. You can find feathers in the garden or out of old pillows or if you are really stuck, they can be bought in haberdashery departments of stores like John Lewis. Don't try to borrow them off the budgie, it won't be appreciated!

You will need a tiny amount of Silver Divisible (DMC ref. No:D283) for the spider's web, or just use a single strand of white if you don't want to buy a whole spool of silver.

STITCHES YOU WILL NEED TO KNOW

Stem (p.35)
Satin (p.29)
Satin Stitch Couching (p.30)
Portuguese Knotted Stem (p.26)
Split (p.35)
Roumanian Couching (p.29)
Turkey Work (p.37)

GENERAL NOTES

Trace the Detailed Outline and transfer it onto your fabric as described in the chapter on General Know-How. Don't bother to trace the detailed bits of the pine cones as they will all be covered with padding.

Use the colour photograph and the Key Diagram to help you follow the instructions.

The shaded areas on the Key Diagram represent all the padded sections. Pad each section as you come to it in the instructions, referring to the particular instructions for Padding with Felt and Bump to help you (p.39).

Read the instructions for any stitches with which you are unfamiliar. Do use the right size and type of needle. It really does make a difference. See the chapter on General Know-How (p.17).

You will probably need a thimble when you come to the pine cones. It's hard work sewing through a lot of padding and a thimble can be an enormous help.

INSTRUCTIONS

Goldcrests

Outline the eyes and the beaks of both birds, using one strand of 310 in tiny Split or Stem stitch. Fill in the eyes and the beaks using one strand of 413 in tiny straight stitches. Make a highlight in each eye, using two strands of Blanc neige in a single Chinese Knot for each eye. Now pad all the sections of the birds represented by shaded areas on the Key Diagram. I used several layers of bump rather than struggling with such tiny little bits of felt, but use whichever method you find easiest. Make the birds quite chubby.

Now do the tops of their heads. For the female bird (see Key Diagram), use two strands of 310 in little straight stitches to fill in the black part of the crown of the head and do the yellow centre using two strands of 725. Do the same for the male bird but add the red bit using two strands of 817.

Now fill in the pale green feathers around the eyes of both birds and down the back of the male bird, using two strands of 3053.

Cover the padding of the breast of the female bird and the cream section of breast showing on the male bird, using three strands of 3047 in Roumanian Couching.

Do the tiny lines of shading on the breast of the female bird (A on the Key Diagram) and outline along the top of the cream coloured breast, where it meets the pale green of the head, using two strands of 3045 in tiny Stem stitch.

Outline the wing section of the female bird. Use the photograph and the Detailed Outline to guide you since your guidelines will have been covered by the padding. Don't worry if your bird's wing is a bit different from mine, it doesn't matter a bit. Use one strand of 310 for the outline and for the black lines of the wing feathers, alternating with one strand of 3053 in Stem stitch lines.

DETAILED OUTLINE

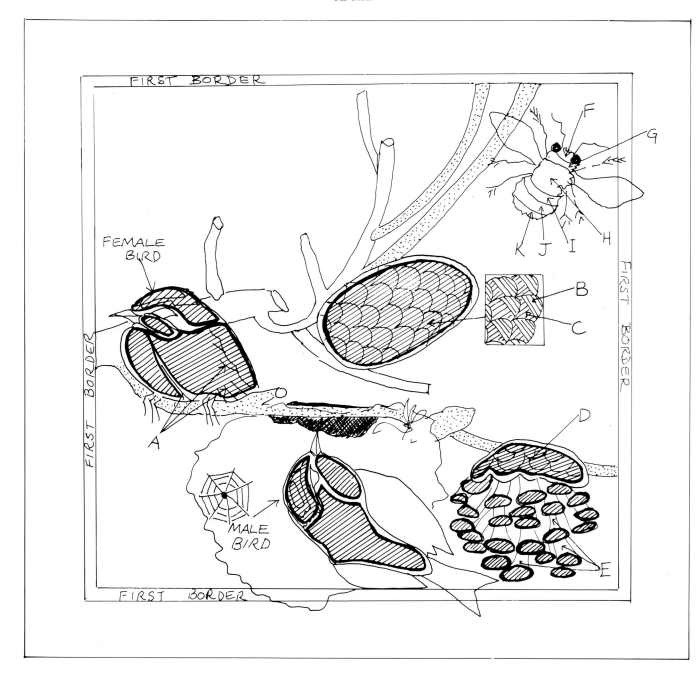

KEY DIAGRAM

Add the two white bands using two strands of Blanc neige in two rows of little straight stitches. Do the wings of the male bird in exactly the same way. Leave his tail until after you have finished the borders, working the tail in long, straight stitch stripes, alternating two strands of 310 with two strands of 3053.

Do the feet of the female bird after you have done the branch.

Corsican Pine

Do the branches first. Use two strands of 3032 mixed with one strand of 3045 for all the branches shaded with dots on the Key Diagram. Use Portuguese Knotted Stem stitch, making just one knot around each of the stem stitches (see the instructions for Portuguese Knotted Stem stitch, p.26, if you are unsure of what I mean). Do all the other branches and all around the first border in two strands of 3045 mixed with one strand of 3031, again in Portuguese Knotted Stem. You can make the two knots around each stem stitch for some of the branches if you want to give them a knobblier look. This is rather a laborious stitch to work but not at all difficult. Just fiddly and takes much longer than ordinary Stem stitch, but does give a much better effect for branches. If you really find it a pain, you could switch to ordinary Stem stitch, for the border but it won't look quite as interesting. See how you feel.

When you have finished the branch upon which the female bird is sitting, you can finish off her little feet, using one strand of 310 in tiny Split stitch.

Cones

Pad the top cone using layers of felt covered in a layer of bump. You will need quite a few layers of the felt to give the cone a good fat shape. If you use too few it will squash flat when you come to lay the covering stitches on top.

Pad the large section of the bottom cone in the same way, and each of the little individual sections (all represented by the shaded areas on the Key Diagram) with two or three stitches of bump for each section. Now finish off the top cone. Draw on top of the padding to guide you or use the photograph and the Detailed Outline to help you. Again, don't worry at all if your end result doesn't exactly match mine. No two pine cones are identical, after all!

You are probably going to hate the next bit as much as I did. It is really hard work getting a needle and thread through all those layers of padding and I must say I resorted to a certain amount of bad temper and teeth grinding and, eventually, a rather strong drink, before I

got to the end. Don't despair, use a thimble, don't grind your teeth and do resort to the strong drink if it helps . . . it certainly numbs the pain of skewering yourself with a sharp needle, I can assure you!

Outline each little section using two strands of 3031 in Stem stitch. Fill in each little diamond shape (see the box on the Key Diagram) with two strands of 731 in little straight stitches for the green half of each diamond (C on the Key Diagram) and two strands of 3032 in straight stitches going the other way (B on the key Diagram) for the beige half of each diamond.

Still sober? If so, carry on . . .!

Now for the second cone. Outline the diamond shapes of the unopened part of the cone (D on the Key Diagram), using two strands of 3031 in Stem stitch, and fill each diamond section using two strands of 3032 in straight, vertical Satin stitch. Now cover each of the other little individually padded sections using two strands of 3032 in Satin stitch.

Fill in the dark brown and black 'stalks' to each little padded section (E on the Key diagram) using two strands of 3031 in Stem stitch and two strands of 310 for the darker bits nearer the base of the cone. (See the photograph to guide you, but again it doesn't matter if you make them more or less shadier than I have).

Pine Needles

This is a lovely, easy bit, to cheer you up after the cone nightmare. I've done all the needles in Stem stitch, using three strands of 469 for some of them and three strands of 731 for the rest. It really doesn't matter which you do in which colour. The needles which cross over the borders and the nest will have to be finished off later.

Bumble-Bee

Outline the legs and the antennae, using one strand of 310 in tiny little Split stitch. Fill in with one strand of 3031 in tiny Satin stitch. Do the eyes in one strand of 310, using two or three little straight stitches for each eye. Outline the wings using one strand of 310 in Stem stitch, leaving the tip of the right wing until you have finished the yellow border. Fill in the left wing (again, you will have to leave the right one until you have done the border) using one strand of 725 in long straight stitches, held in place with one strand of 310 in little stitches for the black veins.

Do the little grey head (F on the Dey Diagram) using one strand of 413 in tiny Satin stitches.

Do the rest of the body in Turkey Work, G on the Key

Diagram in two strands of 725, H in two strands of 310, I in two strands of 725, J in two strands of 310 and K in two strands of Blanc neige. Don't trim the Turkey Work too short until you have finished the whole picture. You can always shorten it then, but if you have made it too short in the first place you won't be able to tidy it up so easily if the bumble-bee gets a bit bedraggled in the course of working the rest of the picture.

Nest

This is the really enjoyable bit.

I've used bits of grey wool, mohair and real feathers and any of the stranded cotton in shades of grey, beige and a bit of green. You can fill in what you want where you want it, with the only proviso that you make a smooth area in a dark shade upon which to add your little spider's web, and that you don't obscure the bird with too much fluff and feather. Work the top entrance to the nest (shaded darkly on the Key Diagram) in 310.

You can embroider little feathers or leaves in any stitches that you happen to know, using two strands of 469 or 413 . . . just have fun with it. Attach the feathers by oversewing their stalky bits with a few invisible stitches. Work bits of wool in a couple of Turkey Work stitches and fluff them up once they are trimmed.

Work the little spider's web (the part of the picture that everyone seems to like best, when they spot it) in a single strand of the Silver Divisible (a ghastly job, separating it . . .sorry) or one strand of Blanc neige if you haven't got any silver. Just work straight stitches for each little line of the web (you will be able to see it more clearly on the Key Diagram) and put a single Chinese Knot in the middle, using two strands of 310, for the spider. I've finished the nest off by outlining the whole thing in two strands of 310 Stem stitch, overlapping the first border where it does it.

Borders

You have already done the first border as part of the pine branches.

Second: Satin Stitch Couching using four strands of bump for the padding, covered with three strands of 725.

Third: Satin Stitch Couching, this time using only two strands of bump for the padding and covering with three strands of 310.

Fourth: Satin Stitch Couching using four strands of bump for the padding, covered with three strands of Blanc neige.

Fifth: finish off with a border of straight Satin stitch using two strands of 817. You will make a neater edge if you first lay a foundation line of Split or Stem stitch along the outside line. Use any left over colour, since it will be covered by the red Satin stitches and you don't want to run out of the red. It's rather a boring chore, laying this foundation line, but does make a tidier finish.

Now finish off all the pine needles that cross over the borders and the nest, the male bird's tail and the bumble-bee's right wing.

May

This picture became my Waterloo. There is no reason why it should be particularly difficult for you, but I think I just went to pieces, having worked so hard on the first four embroideries and knowing that I hadn't even reached the half way mark and had eight more still to do. Imagine!

It was the one I'd been most looking forward to, probably a bad omen in itself, and I'd forgotten that although Turkey Work is quite easy it does take a l . . .o . . .n . . .g time to do. And it did. Boy, did it! I got a complete mental block about finishing the beastly little birds. Poor little things.

I started work on a flight from London to Los Angeles and found that embroidery was a wonderful way to pass the hours of a long 'plane journey. It's much more relaxing than reading and you soon get clever at attaching things like scissors to a ribbon around your wrist so that they can't disappear under the seats, and organising yourself in such a way that your neighbour doesn't get inadvertently skewered with a needle . . . so there I was, thousands of feet up in the sky, struggling with Turkey Work. I was still trying to finish the ducklings on the return journey . . . and for about six weeks after. Hopeless. These awful little half-bald creatures sat there accusingly while I dragged my feet and couldn't get on with it.

I did finish them eventually, of course, and I do think it is one of the nicest pictures. There was absolutely no reason for me to get into such a state about it and no reason on earth for you to do so, unless you too have taken upon yourself the marathon of doing all twelve pictures. If it's your first, you should have a lovely time, especially working the poppies which even I, in my silly mood, found enjoyable. I love that wonderful papery effect that you get, and the way the light catches them and makes them seem full of different shades of red.

The one bit of Turkey Work that I really adored doing was the little furry body of the butterfly. You wait . . . it's just lovely! In fact, I like the butterfly altogether. It would look good on its own, on a collar or something, don't you think? You would have to fill in the little bit of wing-tip that's hidden under the border but that wouldn't be very difficult . . . I think I've just talked myself into it and will have to find a suitable blouse and have a go.

MALLARD DUCKLINGS · *Anas platyrhynchos*
SMALL COPPER BUTTERFLY · *Lycaena phlaes*
FIELD POPPY · *Papaver rhoeas*

70

COLOURS YOU WILL NEED

(DMC Stranded Cotton, 1 skein of each unless otherwise stated)
No. 834 (pale yellow)
No. 310 (black)
No. 3053 (pale green)
No. 469 (darker green)
No. 666 (scarlet)
No. 347 (darker red)
No. 976 (orange)
No. 801 (brown) 2 skeins
DMC Medici wool No. 8303 (ochre)
Bump for padding

STITCHES YOU WILL NEED TO KNOW

Stem (p.35).
Satin (p.29)
Satin Stitch Couching (p.30)
Turkey Work (p.37)
Chinese Knot (p.22)

GENERAL NOTES

Trace the Detailed Outline and transfer it onto your fabric, as described in the chapter on General Know-How (p.17).

Use the colour photograph and the Key Diagram to help you follow the instructions.

This is a relatively easy picture to do. There is very little padding to contend with compared to some of the others and although Turkey Work is rather slow in the making, it's quite fun to do.

Don't be tempted to do the chicks first. All that fluff looks beguiling but you'll only squash the poor little things flat as you continue to work on the rest of the picture.

INSTRUCTIONS

Poppies

Stems: do the stems in Satin Stitch Couching, using three strands of bump for the padding, covered with three strands of 3053. When you get to where the stems meet the border, cut off the bump.

Now do the whole of the first border in Satin Stitch Couching, using four strands of bump for the padding and covering with three strands of 3053. When you come to where the tail of the left hand chick and the breast of the right hand chick will overlap the borders, you will have to stop and start again on the other side (it's too tricky to do the Turkey Work of the chicks on top of the border stitches).

The same goes for where the poppy interrupts the border. I've overlapped the borders on many of these pictures, with leaves and suchlike, but felt that the lovely smoothness of the poppy petals would be spoilt in this case. It's quite tricky finishing off borders at the edge of the petals. Make the edges as neat as you can, pulling the couching Satin stitches down tightly at the very edge to flatten the bump a little more and make less of a stumpy end to your line.

When you come to where the chicks' feet will be, carry straight on. The feet will be laid on top of the border later.

When you come to the ends of the poppy stems, work longer Satin stitches to incorporate the stems and make them look as if they are growing out of the border.

Leaves: Use two strands of 3053 in rows of tiny Stem stitch and then outline the leaves using one strand of 469, again in tiny Stem stitch.

Bud: pad the bud quite fatly, using bump (the heavily outlined, shaded area on the Key Diagram), and cover with one strand of 3053 in Satin stitch, with a line of Stem stitch down the middle.

Flowers: use the Key Diagram to guide you. Outline the petals on the lower flower. All the dotted outlines represent those done in one strand of 666. Outline all the rest, and all of the top flower in one strand of 347, the darker of the two reds. Use tiny Stem stitch.

Now fill in the petals. All the sections of the Key Diagram which are shaded should be filled in with one strand of 347 and all the unshaded areas in one strand of 666. Use rows of tiny Stem stitch, fanning out from the base of the lower flower and the centre of the top flower. It may seem very mean of me to have asked you to use just a single strand, which is obviously a slower process than if you were using two or three, but the finer the Stem stitches are the better you will achieve that wonderful, papery look. When you have finished you will be amazed,

DETAILED OUTLINE

KEY DIAGRAM

as you move the picture so as to catch the light at different angles, at how many shades of red seem to be there, not just the two that you have used. Really gorgeous.

Now do the little black leaves at the top of the stem of the lower flower, using one strand of 310 in tiny Stem stitch. Do the centre of the top flower. Pad the very middle, (A on the Key Diagram) using bump then cover with criss-crossing stitches of one strand of 801 mixed with one strand of 834. Add the Chinese Knots around the centre, doing some of them in one strand of 801 and some in one strand of 310.

Butterfly

Start by filling in the brown bits (shaded with dots on the Key Diagram), using one strand of 801 in Stem stitch.

Don't forget the stripey tail.

Now fill in the black bits (shaded in black on the Key Diagram), using one strand of 310 in tiny Stem stitch for the veins and larger areas and in tiny straight stitches to fill all the awkward little bits. Do the antennae in two tiny, broken lines with a Chinese Knot at the end of each, all in one strand of 310.

Again, don't forget the stripey tail.

Now fill in the orange bits (unshaded on the Key Diagram) using one strand of 976, again in tiny Stem and tiny straight stitches.

This is my favourite bit of the whole picture! . . . the furry body of the butterfly. It's so dark that you may not be able to see clearly in the photograph that the body is done in tiny, furry Turkey Work . . .just the sort of idiotic detail (like the spider's web in the April picture) that pleases me most! Do the top of the head (B on the Key Diagram) using one strand of 801 and the rest of the body (C on the Key Diagram) using one strand of 310, all in miniature Turkey Work. You will have to make closely packed little loops or, when you come to trim it, you will find yourself with a pathetic, balding butterfly! Don't trim it too short until you have finished the whole picture, you don't want to squash the poor creature beyond repair.

Borders

You have already done the first border, as a continuation of the poppies' stems.

As with the first, all subsequent borders will have to stop where they meet the poppy petals and start again on the other side (except for the last border for which you will need simply to shorten your stitches as you work your way around the petal). The same goes for where the chicks' bodies and the tip of the butterfly's wing overlap the borders. Where the chicks feet do so, however, just carry straight on. The feet will be added on top of the border stitches later.

Second: three strands of 310 in Stem stitch.

Third: three strands of 976 in Stem stitch.

Fourth: three strands of 801 in Stem stitch.

Fifth: three strands of 976 in Stem stitch.

Sixth: three strands of 310 in Stem stitch.

Seventh: Satin Stitch Couching, using four strands of bump for the padding, covered in two strands of 347.

Eighth: two strands of 469 in straight Satin stitch. If you want to make a neater edge, go around the whole of the outside line with a foundation line of Stem stitch. It's a boring process, since the line will be covered with the straight Satin stitches, but does make a tidier edge. Use any left-over colour, rather than worry about running out of the green.

Ducklings

Now for the dreaded ducklings. Well, they're not all that dreaded, just rather slow-going.

Outline the eyes and the beaks first (you would never be able to find them if you left them till after the Turkey Working!), using one strand of 310 in tiny Stem stitch. Fill in the pupil of the eyes, again using one strand of 310 in little straight stitches. I haven't filled the beaks in because I thought they showed up better this way. Now do the feet. For each leg, cut off three strands of bump long enough for you to use all three strands to pad the leg, starting nearest the body, and to divide the three strands to use one each for the 'toes'. Don't trim the bump until you reach the tip of each toe or it will become horribly frayed and messy. Overlap the borders where indicated, covering the legs and toes with three strands of 801 in Satin stitch. Fill in the webs with one strand of 834 in long, straight stitches.

Now for the fun of the Turkey Work. It is quite fun, actually . . .ish.

All the black sections of the Key Diagram should be done in three strands of 801.

Make up all the yellow area of each bird using three strands of 834 (pale yellow), two strands of the Medici wool (use a Number 6 needle), or a mixture of two strands of the Medici wool and one strand of 834 (the Number 6 needle should still be big enough). It really doesn't matter where you use which particular colour or texture. I've used the wool/cotton mixture mainly on the breast of the middle bird and left some of the loops untrimmed as an interesting variation on the theme. It's really up to you. If you find the Medici wool tricky to work with, you don't have to use as much as I have, but can substitute more of the pale yellow. See the Turkey Work instructions to help you (p.57).

WRENS · *Troglodytes troglodytes*
RED SQUIRREL . *Sciurus vulgaris*
WILD STRAWBERRIES · *Fragaria vesca*

June

This was my favourite embroidery to work, even though there is a lot to do. It seems to be one of the most popular designs, but the main reason for loving it from my point of view, was that it meant that I had almost reached the haven of the half-way mark, getting as far as June. You cannot imagine how good that was for morale! Having dawdled and procrastinated dreadfully with the poor May ducklings, I raced ahead with enthusiasm. Even the Turkey Worked squirrel's tail went far more quickly than the duckling-fluff.

I've got a best friend called Thomas Birkett, who is six. Thomas only knows a wren when he sees one by its Latin name, *Troglodytes troglodytes*; I taught it to him when he was about three and he thinks it's much more exciting than 'wren'. I agree. I like the fact that such a tiny bird should have such a long Latin name and such an incredibly loud voice to go with it.

My friends the Birketts figure heavily in this picture. Most of it was done at gorgeous weekends spent in their house in Sussex and I remember once asking Thomas's mother, Gloria, what the French was for squirrel. She said, 'Oh, I don't know, something like a rat on wheels, I suppose' . . . well, the French language does have some convoluted ways of saying things! Squirrels are absolutely always known to me now as rats on wheels and June has become the 'Rat on Wheels/*Troglodytes troglodytes*' embroidery!

I hope you will like working this picture as much as I did. There are a few interesting stitches to learn, if you don't already know them. The Striped Woven Band is a very good show-off stitch; make sure you do it when there are non-embroiderers around, they won't half be impressed, I can tell you! It looks so much more difficult than it is, all that business of using two needles at once. I must admit to finding it much easier to work with other people in the room, just so long as they don't know too much and think I'm utterly brilliant. The desire to show off and get a lot done certainly speeds up the work!

I've used the rat on wheels to illustrate the specific instructions for Padding with Felt and Bump (see p.39), so you have got detailed help on how to tackle him . . .or her. You shouldn't have too much trouble and you'll be pleased with the end result.

The wild strawberries are lovely to do. People are fascinated by the way the stems are twined around the border and it's not at all difficult to achieve. The leaves and flowers are really easy, so enjoy yourself.

COLOURS YOU WILL NEED

(DMC Stranded Cotton, 1 skein of each unless otherwise stated)
No. 838 (dark brown)
No. 433 (tan brown)
No. 524 (pale green)
No. 349 (bright red)
No. 744 (yellow)
No. 301 (dark rusty red)
No. 976 (lighter rusty red)
No. 3032 (beige)
No. 3347 (green)
Ecru (cream)
You will need a tiny amount of black to outline the birds' and squirrel's eyes and beaks/nose. Use 310 if you have some handy, or if you don't want to splash out on a whole new skein for the small amount needed, you can get away with ordinary black cotton and no-one will notice.

Bump and Felt for padding.

STITCHES YOU WILL NEED TO KNOW

Stem (p.35)
Satin (p.29)
Satin Stitch Couching (p.30)
Striped Woven Band (p.36)
Detached Overcast (p.23)
Turkey Work (p.37)
Roumanian Couching (p.29)
Chinese Knot (p.22)

GENERAL NOTES

Don't panic and give up before you've started, because of the number of different stitches involved. Even if you don't know a single one of them, if you give yourself time to put in a bit of practice on a separate piece of fabric, before you tackle the picture itself, I think you will find that they are all quite easy stitches to learn and fun to tackle. So, please don't get discouraged. I hardly knew any of the stitches in this book before I started it and if I can do it, you can too.

All the heavily outlined and shaded areas on the Key Diagram represent the sections to be padded. Pad each section as you come to it in the instructions.

When you trace the Detailed Outline and transfer it onto your fabric (p.17), make the lines of the strawberry stalks as faint as possible so that they don't show up under any Detached Overcasting, or leave them out altogether if you feel confident enough to be able to work with the photograph and Detailed Outline to guide you. It's not as tricky as it sounds and it couldn't matter less if your strawberry stalks don't take exactly the same route or cross each other in exactly the same place as mine. Make life easy for yourself and don't feel duty bound to follow me in every tiny detail. Embroidery really should be a pleasant pastime, not a nightmare of worry! You'll probably end up with a much neater picture than mine . . . you certainly couldn't know less about the whole business than I did when I started this book, so if you're a beginner, take heart. And if you're madly experienced, feel smug.

Do use the right size and type of needle. It really does make a difference. See the chapter on General Know-How (p.17).

INSTRUCTIONS

Wrens

Outline the eyes and beaks and 'eyebrows' (A on the Key Diagram), using ordinary black cotton or one strand of 310 if you have it, in tiny Stem stitch. Fill in the pupils of the eyes with tiny straight stitches, again in the single strand of black. Fill in the eyes, the beaks and the 'eyebrows' (do wrens have eyebrows? . . . never mind) using one strand of Ecru in tiny Stem stitch and make a single Chinese Knot for the highlight in each eye, again in the single strand of Ecru.

Outline around the top of the wings and where the backs and heads join (represented by a broken line on the Key Diagram), using two strands of 3032 in tiny Stem stitch.

Now fill in the top of the birds' heads, under the eyes and the backs (B on the Key Diagram) using one strand of 433 mixed with one strand of 838, in tiny Stem stitch lines.

Fill in the birds' white bottoms (C in the Key Diagram) using two strands of Ecru in Stem stitch lines.

Now for the wings. These are made up of Striped Woven Bands. Don't panic if you've never done this stitch before. It's really simple once you've got to grips with it. Read the specific instructions first and practise on another bit of fabric.

Lay the foundation stitches using three strands of 3032.

DETAILED OUTLINE

THIRD
BORDER

E

FIRST BORDER

A

B

C

C

D

B

A

H

F

KEY DIAGRAM

following the lines which you will have already drawn onto your fabric.

Then, starting at the lowest edge of the left hand bird's wing, work the first few rows (represented by the dotted areas on the Key Diagram) in three strands of 3032 threaded in one of your blunt-ended tapestry needles and three strands of 838 threaded in the other. When you have completed four or five lines in that colour scheme, fill in the rest of the wing, sticking to the three strands of 838 in one of your needles and re-threading the second needle with three strands of 433.

Work the wing of the right hand bird in exactly the same way.

Now do the tail of the left hand bird, again in Striped Woven Banding. Lay the foundation stitches, using three strands of 3032. Now thread one of your blunt-ended needles with three strands of 838 and the second with three strands of 3032. Start at the tip of the tail and work five or six rows in that colour scheme. Then, keeping the needle threaded with 838, re-thread the other with three strands of Ecru, to fill in the section represented by the dotted area of tail on the Key Diagram.

Work the tail of the right hand bird the same way but starting with the Ecru/838 combination, to fill in the dotted section of the Key Diagram and changing to the 3032/838 combination for the rest.

Now pad the breasts of both birds (the heavily outlined, shaded sections of the Key Diagram), using little bits of felt built up in layers and covered in bump. See the specific instructions for Padding with Felt and Bump to help you (p.39). Cover the padding in Roumanian Couching, using one strand of Ecru mixed with one strand of 3032. Add the little dark stripes (D on the Key Diagram) using two strands of 838 in rows of little straight stitches. Leave the birds' legs until you have done the strawberry stalks.

Borders

I've worked the first two borders next because so many of the leaves and the tip of the squirrel's tail overlap them. Do the first border in Satin Stitch Couching, using four strands of bump for the padding and covering it with three strands of 3347. When you get to where the strawberry stalks grow up from the border, lengthen a few of your Satin stitches to carry on up the stalks a little way, to make them look as if they are a part of the border.

Now do the second border. You should be familiar with the process of making a Striped Woven band by now.

First, lay down all the little foundation stitches. Don't put a foundation stitch at each of the diagonal (dotted on the Key Diagram) corner lines. Use three strands of Ecru. You really don't need to draw them in first, just make them as evenly spaced as possible. Treat each side of the square as a separate band, working the right hand side first, then the left hand side, then turning the fabric around in your embroidery ring so that the top and then the bottom can also be worked as vertical bands. (At least, I personally found that to be the easiest way). If you lay an even number of foundation lines for each band, you will begin and end the band with the same coloured stripe. If you use an odd number of foundation lines, obviously you will start the band with one colour and end with the other. If you find yourself getting to a corner and stuck with the wrong colour, as I did, naturally, just add an extra, sneaky little foundation stitch and all will be put to rights. I think you will see what I'm getting at as you go along.

Start at the top of the left hand band (E on the Key Diagram). Thread two blunt-ended tapestry needles, one with three strands of Ecru and the other with three strands of 349. Be sure to have enough thread in each needle to get to the end of the band since you can't stop and start a new thread in the middle of a line. If you give yourself double the actual length of the band you should have plenty. Start at E on the Key Diagram and work your way down to F on the Key Diagram.

Finish off and re-thread your needles, then start again at the top. You will need to work about eight or nine rows from top to bottom before you reach the sanctuary of the green, first border, finishing off each time you reach the bottom and re-threading your needles. You are bound to waste some thread but it's better than panicking on the way down that you are going to run out before you reach the end.

Make the stitches at the top and the bottom shorter and shorter as you work inwards so as to keep the diagonal corners. I really can't think of a better way to describe this process. Sorry if it seems awfully wordy, but I thought it better to err on the side of over-explaining rather than to leave you stranded . . . so to speak.

Work each of the other three sides, turning the fabric around in your embroidery ring so as to be able to work the band at the angle you find most convenient.

I should think, by the time you've finished that little lot, you will have had enough of slogging around the borders, so I've moved on to the strawberries at this stage, for a change of scenery, and you can finish the other borders later.

Strawberries

Leaves: Each leaf is made up of one side (darkly shaded on the Key Diagram) in two strands of 3347 slanting Satin stitch, and the other side (unshaded on the Key Diagram) in two strands of 524, also in slanting Satin stitch. Do all the tiny little leaves at the top of each strawberry in the darker green, using just one strand in tiny little straight stitches.

Easy. A relief after that Woven Border, didn't you find?

Flowers: do the green bits of the flowers (have a look at the photograph if you're confused) using two strands of 3347 in tiny straight stitches.

Do the white petals, using two strands of Ecru, in little straight stitches.

Do the centre of each flower, using two strands of 744 in straight stitches, crossing over each other a few times just to pad the centres out a bit. Add the little dots, using one strand of 744 mixed with one strand of 524 in Chinese Knots.

Stems: Use two strands of 524 in Detached Overcast. You can make a sort of Semi-Detached Overcast for the bits of stem that don't need to cross either the border or themselves. It's a dreadfully fiddly stitch to work, Detached Overcast, but the end result is marvellous. I promise you, people will marvel at those squiggling little tendrils curling around the borders and each other.

Berries: pad each strawberry with three or four criss-crossing stitches of bump, to make them nice and fat. Then, using two strands of 349, go around the circumference of each strawberry in Stem stitch and fill in the middles in straight stitches. Cover the padding well with the red or you will find the little dots which you are about to add on top will disrupt the underlying stitches. Mix two strands of Ecru with one strand of 524 and scatter seven or eight tiny little stitches over each strawberry, for the 'dots'. Don't pull these little stitches too tight or they will disappear into the red. It's quite hard work getting through the padding.

Squirrel

Outline the eye with one strand of Ecru in Stem stitch. Fill in the black pupil with one strand of 310 in straight stitches. Make the black 'eyebrow' (G on the Key Diagram) using one strand of 310 in a line of Stem stitch. Make the highlight of the eye with a single Chinese Knot, using one strand of Ecru.

Make the little nose and mouth with one strand of 310 in tiny little straight stitches.

Do the white outline of the squirrel's left ear, using one strand of Ecru.

Do the black line inside the ear (H on the Key Diagram) using one strand of 310 in Stem stitch.

Fill in the rest of both right and left ear, using two strands of 301 in Stem stitch with a few straight stitches for the tufts.

Fill in the rest of the unpadded section of the head using two strands of 976 in rows of Stem stitch

Now do all the padded sections of the squirrel. Pad the two little fat bits either side of the mouth, the cheek, body, chest, underbelly and legs. Use bump on its own for the small areas and layers of felt covered with bump for the body. Make the squirrel good and fat. See the specific instructions for Padding with Felt and Bump, to help you (p.39).

Now cover the little fat bits on either side of the mouth using two strand of Ecru in little straight stitches.

Cover the cheek and any bits of face that you have not already done in the lighter rust colour, using two strands of 301 in Roumanian Couching.

Cover the white breast and underbelly, using two strands of Ecru in Roumanian Couching.

Cover the whole of the body and the legs with one strand of 301 mixed with one strand of 976 in Roumanian Couching. Do the feet in the same colour mixture, using straight stitches and going over the border with the near front and hind feet.

Tail: do the whole tail in Turkey Work. All the areas of the tail shaded on the Key Diagram with dots are done in one strand of 838 mixed with one strand of 301. The rest of the tail is done in three strands of 976. Carry on straight through the border stitches where the tail crosses over the borders, not easy but not all that difficult, either. Don't trim the tail too short until you have finished the last of the borders, or you might squash it beyond repair as you go along. You can always crop it shorter if you've left yourself enough to play with.

Borders

You have already done the first border, in green, and the second, Striped Woven Border.

Third: do a border of Satin Stitch Couching, using four strands of bump for the padding. Cover the left and right sides with three strands of 3032 and the top and bottom with three strands of 433.

Fourth: straight Satin stitch, using two strands of 744. If you want to make a nice, neat edge, first lay a foundation line of Stem stitch all the way round the outside edge, in any of the pale colours that you have left over rather than using up your supply of 744 and worrying about running out of it. It's a chore, since this foundation line will be covered with the Satin stitches, but does make for a tidier edge.

DIPPER · *Cinclus cinclus*
DRAGONFLY · *Somatochlora metallica*
MARSH FROG · *Rana ridibunda*

July

I had passed the magical half-way mark by the time I got to July, and become more and more obsessed along the way with the whole business of using padding to make these creatures as life-like as possible. It's lucky that there are only twelve months in the year; if I'd done many more, they would have become completely three-dimensional sculptures by the end, and have parted company with the fabric altogether!

I like the fragility and transparency of the dragonfly, by way of contrast to the heavy padding of the frog and dipper . . . (it sounds like a pub, doesn't it? The 'Frog and Dipper'.)

It is often the way, that a design in which one has had no particular confidence, turns out to be one of the best . . . and, unhappily, sometimes vice versa. This is one of those that I wasn't at all sure about when I started and now I put it firmly amongst my favourites. I love the shinyness of the frog and the smooth pebbles and I was thrilled to find the glittering metallic thread for the dragonfly. You don't have to use it, as I have explained in the instructions, if you don't want to be extravagant. It is more expensive than ordinary stranded cotton, but I do think it is worth the extra cost to achieve that wonderful dragonfly quality.

Did you know that dippers can walk along a river under the water in search of food? They dive to the bottom and walk upstream, keeping their heads down in search of passing water-boatmen or delicacies like dragonfly nymphs, and the current against their backs stops them bobbing up to the surface. Fascinating, don't you think?

The feet are a bit difficult to do, getting through the thick padding of the stone, but the rest of the bird is pretty straightforward.

Frogs are lucky for me. I've always loved them. When I was little there was a pond near the house we have in France, that was always full of tiny, shiny tree frogs; if you held a stick over the pond, they would hop onto it and cling on with their fat little fingers. It was such a thrill and I've loved frogs ever since. I have a jade one which my father bought in China before I was born, and a tiny Ashanti gold weight in the shape of a frog; they both go everywhere with me, constantly being swopped about from handbag to evening bag and so on.

This particular picture is dedicated to my friend Emilia Fox, whose birthday is in July.

DETAILED OUTLINE

COLOURS YOU WILL NEED

(DMC Stranded Cotton, 1 skein of each, unless otherwise stated)
No. 433 (rusty brown)
No. 503 (pale green)
No. 731 (bright green
No. 935 (dark green)
No. 932 (pale blue)
No. 796 (dark blue)
No. 414 (grey)
No. 744 (yellow)
No. 310 (black)
No. 3031 (dark brown)
No. 3032 (beige)
Blanc neige (white)
1 spool of Silver Divisible (DMC ref. no: D283)
    Elizabeth Stuart Cord No.21 (metallic emerald green). This metallic thread is wonderful and gives the dragonfly its shimmery look, but it is rather expensive. If you don't feel like being extravagant, then you can substitute DMC's Stranded Cotton No. 909 mixed with a strand of the Silver Divisible for the shiny effect. It won't be quite as exciting as the metallic look, but you will still have a dragonfly at the end.
    Bump and Felt for padding.

STITCHES YOU WILL NEED TO KNOW

Stem (p.35)
Satin (p.29)
Satin Stitch Couching (p.30)
Roumanian Couching (p.29)
Chinese Knot (p.22)

GENERAL NOTES

Trace the Detailed Outline and transfer it onto your fabric as described in the chapter on General Know-How (p.17). Don't bother to trace and transfer those details that will later be covered with padding: the bird's feet, the markings on the frog and the parts of its leg and feet that go across the stone.

    Use the colour photograph and the Key Diagram to help you follow the instructions.

    The shaded areas on the Key Diagram represent all the padded sections. Don't try and fill in all the padding first, do each section as you come to it in the instructions. Read the specific instructions for Padding with Felt and Bump to help you (p.39).

    Read the instructions for any stitch with which you are unfamiliar.

    Do use the right size and type of needle. It really does make a difference. See the chapter on General Know-How (p.17).

    Use a thimble to help you sew through the padding.

INSTRUCTIONS

Stones

Start by padding the stones. You will need several layers of felt to make them good and fat, covered with a layer of bump. Now thread two needles, one with one strand of 414 and the other with three strands of 414. Cover the stones with long straight stitches using the three strands of 414 and hold each long stitch in place as you go along with a few slanting couching stitches, using the single strand of 414. Make these couching stitches as invisible as possible so that the effect when you have finished is as smooth and shiny as possible. Do both stones in exactly the same way.

Dipper

Do the bird's eye first. Outline it, using one strand of 310 in tiny Stem stitch. Use one strand of 744 for the inside, yellow ring, again in tiny Stem stitch. Fill in the pupil, using one strand of 310 in little straight stitches and make a single Chinese Knot using one strand of Blanc neige for the highlight.

    Beak: outline the beak with one strand of 310 and fill in the lower half of the beak with the same, all in tiny Stem stitch. Fill in the upper mandible (A on the Key diagram) in one strand of Blanc neige, again in tiny Stem stitch.

    Now pad the whole of the breast area (heavily outlined and shaded on the Key Diagram.) You will need several layers of felt covered with a layer of bump. Don't worry that you are covering up your guidelines for where the feathers change from white to brown to dark brown. You can draw these lines in again on top of the bump if you need them, or just use the photograph and Detailed Outline to remind you of what to do. It doesn't matter in

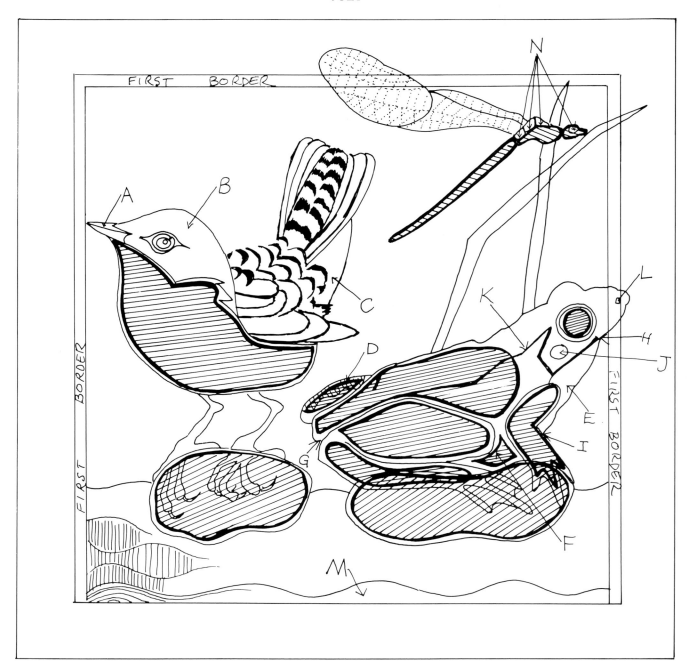

KEY DIAGRAM

the least if your feathers don't go in exactly the same place as mine.

Start at the beak and cover all of the white part of the breast using three strands of Blanc neige in Roumanian Couching. Then change to the rusty brown colour, using three strands of 433, again in Roumanian Couching. Then change to the dark brown, using three strands of 3031, again in Roumanian Couching.

Now fill in the head (section B on the Key diagram) using three strands of 433 in Stem stitch.

Feathers: Outline all the feathers and fill in the black sections (all marked in black on the Key Diagram) using two strands of 310 in Stem stitch and little straight stitches. I used just one strand to outline the long tail feathers. Now mix one strand of 3031 with one strand of 444 and fill in all the feathers: use rows of Stem stitch for the long tail feathers, little straight stitches for all the little feathers on the birds back and up the centre of the tail, and slanting Satin stitch for the larger wing feathers. Fill in under the tail (section C on the Key Diagram) using two strands of 3031 in rows of Stem stitch.

Legs and feet: Draw guidelines for the feet on top of the bump, if it helps you, or just use the photograph and Detailed Outline to remind you of how they should go. Don't worry a bit if your bird's feet aren't exactly the same as my bird's feet. As long as he's perching on the stone, it really couldn't matter less if the feet are slightly different. Mix one strand of 3031 with one strand of 433. Take three strands of bump and, starting at the top of one leg, nearest the body, cover the three strands of the bump with the 3031/433 mixture. When you get to the feet, separate the bump and use one strand to pad each toe, continuing to cover in the 3031/433 mixture. It's a bit of a nightmare getting through the thick padding of the stone. Take your time, try not to swear as much as I did and use a thimble if it helps drive your needle through the stone rather than through your finger. Do the same with the other foot. Add the claws using one strand of 310 in tiny Stem stitch.

Borders

You don't have to do all the borders in one go if you find it awfully boring slogging around the edges over and over again, but it does help to get them out of the way at this stage since bits of the frog, the dragonfly's wing and the tips of the grasses overlap. See how you feel. You can always move on and do the frog's legs or the dragonfly's

body for a bit of a breather from the borders, if you feel inclined. Here, anyway, are instructions for all of the borders.

For the first border, work just three sides of the square, leaving the water to make up the bottom line, as illustrated. Use four strands of bump and cover with three strands of 932 in Satin Stitch Couching. All the subsequent borders go around all four sides of the frame.

Second: three strands of 796 in Stem stitch.
Third: two strands of Blanc neige in Stem stitch.
Fourth: three strands of 414 in Stem stitch.
Fifth: three strands of 731 in Stem stitch.
Sixth: three strands of 935 in Stem stitch.
Seventh: three strands of 433 in Stem stitch.
Eighth: three strands of 3031 in Stem stitch.
Ninth: Satin Stitch Couching using four strands of bump for the padding covered with three strands of 503.
Tenth: three strands of 744 in Stem stitch.
Eleventh: three strands of 796 in Stem stitch.
Twelfth: finish off the frame with a border of straight Satin stitch, using two strands of 3032. You will achieve a tidier edge if you first lay a foundation line of Stem stitch using two strands of 744 (you will only need to save a little of the pale yellow for the frog's eyes and I don't want you to run out of the 3032 which will cover this foundation line). Don't worry if your border lines aren't too perfectly straight. As you can see, it's not something that worries me a lot!

Frog

Pad all the sections of the frog represented by the heavily outlined, shaded areas on the Key Diagram. It's a bit strange to be adding more padding on top of the stone padding, in the case of the legs, but you'll manage, I'm sure. Draw the outline of the near hind and front legs on top of the stone if it helps you, or refer to the Detailed Outline and the photograph to remind you of what goes where. Make the frog really fat and juicy, and make the eye really bulgey.

Now cover the legs. Use three strands of 731 in smooth straight Satin stitches to cover the front and near-hind legs and toes. Cover the little bit of the rear-hind leg in three strands of Blanc neige, then add the green section (cross-hatched, marked D and still rather hard to see on the Key Diagram) on top of the Blanc neige stitches. Use straight Satin stitches, as with the other two legs.

Fill in the webbing of the back foot using two strands of 935 in straight stitches.

Fill in the throat (E on the Key Diagram) and cover the little bit of belly showing (F on the Key Diagram), both in two strands of Blanc neige, the throat in Stem stitch lines and the belly in straight stitches to cover the padding.

Now cover the bulgey eye. Cover the whole eye with three strands of 744 and add the central black part on top with three strands of 310, all in long straight stitches. They tend to slither down the mound of padding to start with, and you can add little couching stitches to keep them in place, if you want to. I found that, by the time I had laid enough stitches across, they managed to stay in place on their own. See how you get on. Make a ring of Stem stitch, using two strands of 731 around the circumference of the eye.

Now do the body. Outline from G to H on the Key Diagram, using three strands of 935 in Stem stitch. Outline from H to I on the Key Diagram, using one strand of 731, again in Stem stitch.

Now cover the rest of the body. Using three strands of 935, take long, straight stitches right across the length of the body from the tail to the edge of the eye and from the other side of the eye to the tip of the nose. Fill in the whole of the dark green area in this way (have a look at the colour photograph to help you). Keep these long stitches in place by adding the black spots (see the Detailed Outline where they are represented, funnily enough, as black spots) using two strands of 310 and the little green knobbles (represented by little unshaded circles on the Detailed Outline), in Chinese Knots made up of two strands of 935. It doesn't matter where you scatter these knots, just put them wherever the long stitches of the foundation colour look as if they need fixing in place. Fill in the three white spots just above the knee of the hind leg (have a look at the photograph to show you which particular spots I mean), using two strands of Blanc neige in little straight stitches. Fill in the big spot marked with a J on the Key Diagram, and do the line marked with a K, both using three strands of 731. Do the J spot in little straight stitches and the K line in Stem stitch. This line will also serve to keep the long body stitches in place. Make a little single stitch for the nostril (L on the Key Diagram), again using three strands of 731.

Add the stripes and spots on the legs in three strands of 310. Use straight stitches and try not to disturb the smoothness of the background colour. It's hard work, again, going through all the padding, but keep at it and don't worry if your stripes and spots aren't in exactly the same place as mine. Use the Detailed Outline and the photograph to remind you of roughly where they should go.

Water

Use three strands of 932 in Stem stitch to follow the wavy lines and to fill in the whole of the section marked M on the Key Diagram.

You will, no doubt, hate doing the wavy lines that go right across the stones just as much as I did. I was in the most awful temper by the time I had stabbed my fingers a few times and I stopped for a strong cup of tea (or something even stronger) when I'd got through that little hurdle. Not amusing! Fill in the dark blue of the water using three strands of 796 in straight, vertical lines. See the little shaded section in the bottom left-hand corner of the Key Diagram to help you.

Blades of Grass

Use two strands of 503 in Stem stitch lines. Do the right-hand, straight blade first, filling it in completely, even where the dragonfly and the other blade will cross it and overlapping the border. Now fill in the other blade, crossing over the first one and overlapping the border.

Dragonfly

Legs: use one strand of 310 in tiny Stem stitch for each leg and add the little spikey hairs in tiny straight stitches.

Body: pad the body and tail, using six strands of one of the green colours, whatever is left over. It's a bit less clumsy for such small areas than using bump.

Cover the tiny little areas indicated by the N on the Key Diagram, using two strands of 3032 in tiny straight stitches.

Cover the rest of the body and head with the Elizabeth Stuart Cord No.21. if you are using it, or two strands of 909 mixed with one strand of the Silver Divisible, if you haven't got the metallic green. See the specific instructions for Using Metal Thread (p.40) if you want to do it the proper way, or else cheat, as I did, and use the metal thread as you would the ordinary kind, working straight stitches to cover the padding.

Cover the tail, again with the metallic thread if you are using it, or the 909/Silver version. If you do use the metallic thread, it would be helpful to do it the proper way. Have a look at the specific instructions for Using Metal Thread (p.40). Use two strands of 310 to keep the threads in place and form the lines marking the divisions of each section of the tail.

Wing: I've saved what I thought was the nastiest bit till last. Outline with one strand of 3032 in tiny, tiny Stem stitch, all those lines not represented by dots on the Key Diagram.

This is the bit I really loathed: separate up the Silver Divisible into individual strands. I don't know if I was being particularly stupid, but I found this to be a task of mind-boggling fiddlesomeness.

Now fill in all the tiny little criss-crossings marked as dotted lines on the Key Diagram. I took the thread in and out of the fabric, which you are not, strictly speaking, supposed to do. You'll know that if you've looked up the instructions for Using Metal Thread. Still, it's not so difficult to cheat a bit, and I couldn't be bothered with all that couching. You just do whatever you feel like.

BARN OWL · *Tyto alba*
HARVEST MOUSE · *Micromys minutus*
COMMON WHEAT · *Triticum vulgare*

August

I love these ghostly birds. I've seen them occasionally in Sussex, hunting at dusk on an early evening in autumn. Thrilling. I did a rather stylized tawny owl and its chick for one of my little practice samplers which you can see in the Introduction to this book and copy if you feel like using it, as I did, as a way of getting used to lots of unfamiliar stitches. When it came to designing the August picture, though, I decided that the tawny owl and chick were rather too cartoony and out of keeping with the other eleven, so the obvious alternative was to do a barn owl.

I must say that it was a perfect nightmare to design. I used Eric Hosking's fabulous book, *Owls*, published by Pelham, to show me quite brilliantly how they ought to look, and although nothing is as ravishing as the real thing, I think the strange quality of the embroidery does go some way towards a good barn owl feel. It would be silly to pretend that it is a particularly easy picture to work. It's not, but it is a great deal easier to embroider than it was to draw, so take heart! I've used this barn owl as the example in the specific instructions for Semi-Detached Buttonhole Stitch and done my level best to describe every little detail of the process as clearly as possible, so that you don't get into a state over it. You need not learn Rope Stitch for the wing feathers, if you can't face it. Slanting Satin Stitch will do perfectly well as an alternative.

The wheat doesn't present any great difficulties, and as for the mighty mouse . . .did you know that barn owls can hunt in complete darkness, by their sense of hearing? They have asymmetrical ears that pick up sound at fractional intervals so that they can pin-point their prey accurately. I think the mouse in this picture is so huge that it would get caught even if the owl wore ear muffs, although, as I've said in the instructions, the bird would probably choke if he did catch it.

Feel free, as with all the embroideries in this book, to substitute stitches if you get really stuck. Don't bother to use Rope Stitch for the border if you haven't used it for the owl. If you know other interesting border stitches, do use them anywhere you want to. My suggestions are just there because it was the way I wanted to work the borders, and as a guide. You don't have to stick to them if you want to be more adventurous. I should keep roughly to the same colour scheme, and don't forget that if you do use different stitches, that you might need more or less thread than I have allowed for, as they will use up different amounts.

DETAILED OUTLINE

COLOURS YOU WILL NEED

(DMC Stranded Cotton, 1 skein of each unless otherwise stated)
No. 834 (light golden)
No. 729 (medium golden)
No. 680 (darker golden)
No. 435 (light tan)
No. 869 (brown)
No. 414 (grey)
No. 731 (green)
No. 224 (pink)
No. 310 (black)
No. 3047 (light beige) 2 skeins
Blanc neige (white)
Bump and Felt for padding.

STITCHES YOU WILL NEED TO KNOW

Stem (p.35)
Satin (p.29)
Satin Stitch Couching (p.30)
Roumanian Couching (p.29)
Rope (optional, but worth it) (p.28)
Detached Overcast (p.23)
Semi-Detached Buttonhole (p.31)
Raised Fishbone (p.27)
Chinese Knot (p.22)

GENERAL NOTES

Don't panic and give up before you've started at the thought of all those stitches. Even if you don't know any of them, they are all much easier than they look and I'm absolutely confident that my brilliantly explicit and detailed stitch instructions will make the learning process enjoyable. Seriously!

Trace the Detailed Outline onto your fabric, but don't trace the mouse's tail or the details on its body, or the little grey stripes on the owl's wings. All these details will be covered up later on by padding or foundation stitches. Don't panic at that thought either; you can use the photograph and the Detailed Outline to guide you and even draw on top of the padding if it helps. It's not that difficult. All the heavily outlined and shaded areas on the Key Diagram represent the padded sections. I haven't bothered to shade every single little bit of wheat, I'm sure

you will understand from the one on the right, that all the others are done in the same way.

Do use the right size and type of needle. It really does make a difference. See the Chapter on General Know-How (p.17).

INSTRUCTIONS

Mouse

A friend of mine rudely says that this mouse has taken on the proportions of a coypu (if you know what that is . . .anyway, it's a rodent as big as a beaver and very useful in crosswords). Well, if you look through this book you will see that I have paid absolutely no attention whatsoever to scale anywhere, so you'll have to bear with this mega-mouse. I like him. And at least there's very little chance of his getting caught . . .I think the owl would choke!

Onwards . . . Pad the mega-mouse's mega-body, using layers of felt covered with bump. See the specific instructions for Padding with Felt and Bump (p.39) to help you.

Cover the underbelly and throat (the dotted shading on the Key Diagram) with one strand of Blanc neige mixed with one strand of 414 in long Stem stitches.

Cover the legs with two strand of 435 in Roumanian Couching for the big, near foreleg and little Satin stitches for the others.

Leave the pink feet and tail till later.

Cover the rest of the body with two strands of 435 mixed with one strand of 869, in Roumanian Couching.

Add the eye, ear, nose and mouth using one strand of 310 in Stem stitch and little straight stitches. Add the whiskers, again using one strand of 310 in little straight stitches.

Borders

You can either do all of the borders at this stage, or, if you find all that slogging around too boring keep at it until you have got as far as finishing the sixth and then move on to the next stage, returning to the borders at the end. It's up to you. I personally quite like finishing all the borders at this stage, but it's not compulsory. Do get to the sixth, though, as the owl's wings overlap as far as that point.

Do the first border in Satin Stitch Couching. Start at point A on the Key Diagram. Use two strands of 680 mixed with two strands of 731 to cover the bump as far as point B

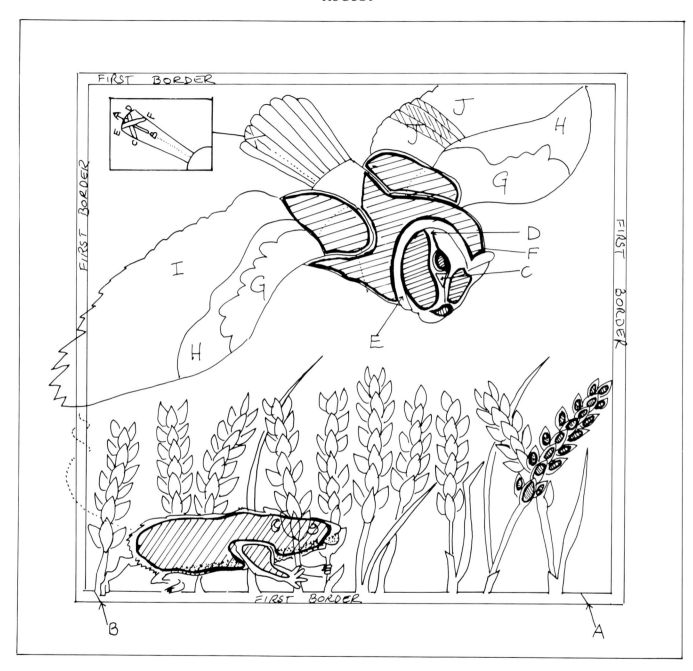

KEY DIAGRAM

on the Key Diagram, including carrying on the stitching up the (unpadded) stalks and leaves of the wheat, as you get to them.

When you finally reach point B, change the covering colour to three strands of 729 and work your way all the way round, continuing on your way where the owl's wing will later overlap the border, until you reach point A again.
Second: use three strands of 869 in Stem stitch.
Third: three strands of 731 in Stem stitch.
Fourth: three strands of 680 in Stem stitch.
Fifth: three strands of 731 in Stem stitch.
Sixth: Satin Stitch Couching, using four strands of bump for the padding, covered with three strands of 310.

Stop border-stitching at this point, if you've had enough and resume later. If you want to go on . . .
Seventh: three strands of 224 in Stem stitch.
Eighth: Satin Stitch Couching using only three strands of bump for the padding, covered with three strands of 414.
Ninth: use Rope stitch if you decided to master it for the owl's wings, or Satin stitch if you didn't. Do the left and right hand sides in three strands of 834 and the top and bottom in three strands of 869. If you are using Rope stitch you will have to cheat a bit at the corners; you'll see what I mean when you get there and find the slant of the stitch going the wrong way. Just add a few little extra Satin stitches, fanning round to make up the join and don't worry about it.

Wheat

Pad each little section of wheat with a single stitch of bump, as represented by the shaded sections of the stem on the far right of the Key Diagram. Cover these little padded sections, starting with the stem on the far left of the picture, using three strands of 729 in little Satin stitches. Do the next stem using three strands of 834 and carry on along the line, alternating the two colours. Where the fourth stem from the left crosses over the mouse, just go over the mouse as if it wasn't there . . . except that you'll be well aware that it is because it is pretty heavy-going, getting through all that padding.

Finish off the tail and feet of the mouse. For the feet, use two strands of 224 in tiny straight stitches, working over the stems of the wheat where the feet are holding on. Use one strand of 310 in tiny stitches between each toe so that they show up better.

For the tail, use three strands of 224 in Detached Overcast, referring to the photograph and Detailed Outline to remind yourself of how it goes.

Owl

Pad the areas of the face represented by the heavily outlined, shaded sections on the Key Diagram, using two layers of bump. A couple of stitches of bump will do for the beak, and overlay three or four for the eye.

Cover and outline the eye, using one strand of 310 in straight stitches across the padding and tiny Stem stitches along the top line.

Make a Chinese Knot using two strands of Blanc neige, for the highlight in the pupil.

Make a few stitches in the corner of the eye (C on the Key Diagram) using two strands of 680.

Cover the beak using two strands of 3047 in Satin stitch and add a tiny stitch each side of the beak in one strand of 310 for the nostrils.

Fill in the rest of the white face using two strands of Blanc neige in Satin stitch, starting at the top of the beak and laying the stitches in the directions represented by the shading lines on the Detailed Outline. Carry on around the heart-shape of the face, changing to one strand of Blanc neige mixed with one strand of 3047 as you get past the outside corner of the eye (D on the Key Diagram) and carrying on until you reach the beak again.

Now do the edge of the heart-shape (E on the Key Diagram). Take two strands of bump to pad it out a bit and cover with one strand of 680 mixed with one strand of 3047 in Satin Stitch Couching.

Body: pad the sections of the body represented by the heavily outlined, shaded areas on the Key Diagram. Use little layers of felt covered with bump, or layers of bump on its own, whichever you prefer. Make the three sections quite chubby, leaving distinct divisions between each section.

Now have a good look at the specific instructions for Semi-Detached Buttonhole (p.31) where I have described exactly how the owl is done. I just felt that I could take more space and usefully describe the stitch itself in that section of the book rather than here.

Your starting point is marked F on the Key Diagram.

Again, have a good look at the specific instructions for Semi-Detached Buttonhole to help you with the Semi-Detached wing sections.

Fill the two sections marked G on the Key Diagram with closely bunched feathers using two strands of 435 mixed with one strand of 3047.

Fill the two sections marked H on the Key Diagram with closely bunched feathers using three strands of 3047. I think these Semi-Detached feathers are simply wonderful, it's such an interesting texture.

Now do the long wing feathers. Do all those in section J of the Key Diagram in slanting Satin stitch using one strand of Blanc neige mixed with one strand of 3047. Slant the stitches in the direction illustrated by the three representative feathers detailed in section J on the Key Diagram.

For section I on the Key Diagram, work each feather in Rope stitch, if you know it or feel like learning a lovely, new stitch, or in Satin again if you don't. Again, use one strand of Blanc neige mixed with one strand of 3047.

Now lay the little grey stripes on top of each of the long wing feathers. Use the photograph to guide you as to where they go; I didn't mark them all on the Key Diagram or Detailed Outline because I thought it would be confus-

ing. The photograph should give you a good enough guide. Use two strands of 414 and make two little stitches in a V shape for each little stripe.

Tail: again, use one strand of Blanc neige mixed with one strand of 3047, but this time do each tail feather in Raised Fishbone stitch. The inset box detail, representing one feather from the tail, shows you how to start off, which will make sense when you look at the specific instructions for Raised Fishbone.

Add the little grey feathers using two strands of 414 in little V shapes going against the grain of the feather. Have a look at the photograph to guide you.

Now finish off the borders if you didn't do so earlier, following the instructions already given.

September

The bulrush was one of the first things I had a go at practising. I wasn't quite sure how to make that strange texture and then hit upon the Chinese Knots idea. I think these little knots, which are a perfect pain to do in such quantity, are nevertheless exactly appropriate.

I had already discovered Elizabeth Stuart's miraculous metallic threads when I was working on the dragonfly in the July picture, and couldn't wait to use the blue for the kingfisher. What exquisite birds they are. I don't think that there is any representation quite as beautiful as the real thing, but the blue metallic thread does go a long way to showing the shimmering quality of these jewel-like birds.

Do you know the mythology surrounding kingfishers? If you don't, it's worth telling here, and if you do, it's nice to be reminded.

The Latin name for a kingfisher is *Alcedo atthis*. In Ovid's version of the legend of Ceyx and Alcyone, Ceyx is drowned in a shipwreck, the gods take pity on his distraught wife Alcyone and turn them both into kingfishers so that they can still be together. The Greek word for a kingfisher is *halkyon*, from *hals* (sea) and *kyon* (conceive). Alcyone always nested at the edge of the sea and in the week before and the week after the winter solstice, Zeus would calm the turbulent waters so that Alcyone could hatch her chicks safely. And that is why we refer to calm and peaceful times as 'halcyon days'.

Back to earth. The feet are my favourite things in this picture. I love the kingfisher's little orange feet and I think the otter has a wonderful slithery wet look. The otter is quite easy to do. You might find that embroidering the bulrush leaves which cross over his tail is a bit tough, but it isn't really difficult.

The only tricky part of the picture is the double padding of the bird's beak overlaying the bulrushes. I like the look of all those crossings over, but it is slightly fiddly making the beak lie evenly and not go up and down over the hump of the bulrush. Just keep on adding bump until you have a smooth surface.

Don't feel obliged to follow exactly what I have done for the borders. You could easily substitute other stitches in your repertoire if you feel adventurous, but don't forget that different stitches use up different amounts of thread and that you may need more or less than I have allowed for.

COMMON KINGFISHER · *Alcedo atthis*
OTTER · *Lutra lutra*
BULRUSH · *Typha latifolia*

SEPTEMBER

COLOURS YOU WILL NEED

(DMC Stranded Cotton, 1 skein of each unless otherwise stated)
No. 733 (yellowy green)
No. 469 (green)
No. 433 ('otter' brown)
No. 646 (grey)
No. 932 (pale blue)
No. 792 (purply-blue)
No. 924 (dark greeny-blue)
No. 301 (orangey-brown)
No. 976 (lighter orangey-brown)
No. 612 (beige)
No. 310 (black)
No. 3031 (dark brown)
Ecru (cream)
Elizabeth Stuart Cord No. 27. This is the wonderful metallic blue that I have used for the Kingfisher's head and wing. It's expensive and if you don't want to splash out on such an extravagance, you could substitute DMC Stranded Cotton No. 796, but you won't get the lovely, shiny effect. I personally think that it is well worth it, but don't worry if you do want to opt for the stranded cotton. You will still have a kingfisher at the end of it all.

STITCHES YOU WILL NEED TO KNOW

Stem (p.35)
Roumanian Couching (p.29)
Satin Stitch Couching (p.30)
Chinese Knot (p.22)
Couched Metal Thread (see Using Metal Thread) (p.40)

GENERAL NOTES

Trace the Detailed Outline and transfer it onto your fabric as described in the chapter on General Know-How (p.17).

Use the colour photograph and the Key Diagram to help you follow the instructions.

All the heavily outlined and shaded areas on the Key Diagram represent the padded sections of the picture. Pad each section as you come to it in the instructions, using the specific instructions for Padding with Felt and Bump to help you (p.39).

Read the instructions for any stitches with which you are unfamiliar Do use the right size and type of needle. It really does make a difference. See the chapter on General Know-How (p.17).

This is a relatively easy picture to work. Don't panic and feel put off if you don't know some of the stitches. I didn't either when I started this book and they really aren't too difficult to learn . . . thanks to my brilliant stitch instructions, of course!

INSTRUCTIONS

Bulrushes

Leaves: Where the leaves overlap each other, completely fill in the underlying one first and then do the overlying one, going straight through the underlying leaf's stitches. See the Detailed Outline for which goes where.

Fill in all the lighter coloured leaves and stalks (all those shaded with dots on the Key Diagram) using two strands of 733 in rows of Stem stitch.

Fill in all the darker green leaves and stalks using two strands of 469, again in rows of Stem stitch.

All those leaves that overlap the border and the otter's tail will have to be left till later.

Now pad the fat, dark brown parts of the bulrushes, A and B on the Key Diagram. Use two layers of bump for each, one layer made up of two long stitches going from top to bottom and the next of closely laid stitches going the other way, to cover the first layer. Now cover all of this padding and the whole of the unpadded bulrush (C on the Key Diagram), in Chinese Knots made up of two strands of 3031 mixed with one strand of 310. It's awfully slow work and you'll have to be careful not to let the knots disappear down between the bump stitches, hence the need to pack these closely together in the first place.

For the little spikes at the top of each (D, E and F on the Key Diagram), use one strand of 612 in Stem stitch. You'll have to leave the bits of D and E which overlap the borders until later.

Kingfisher

Outline the eye and fill in the pupil, using two strands of 310 in Stem stitch. Make a highlight in the pupil using two strands of Ecru in a single Chinese Knot. Fill in the whites of the eye, again in the two strands of Ecru, in little straight stitches.

Pad the top of the head and the beak (outlined heavily and shaded on the Key Diagram), using bump; you will

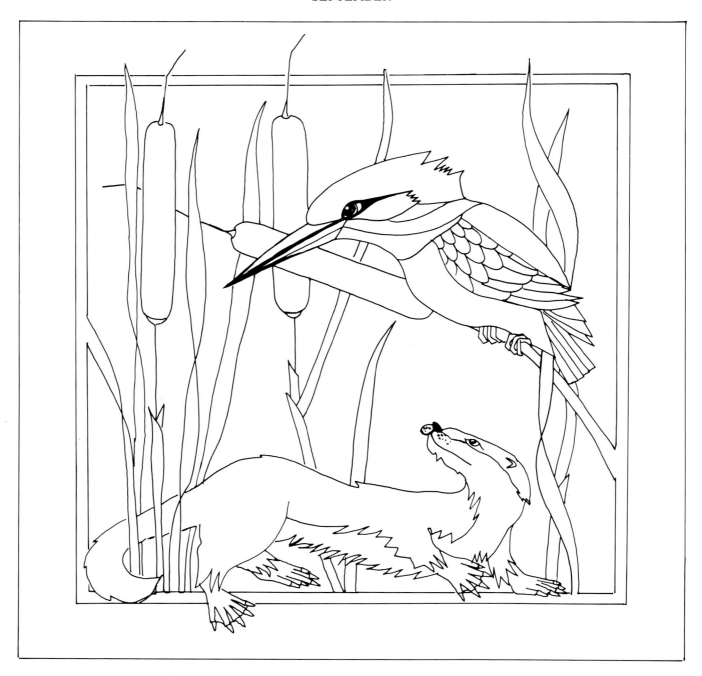

DETAILED OUTLINE

have to pad the beak quite fatly to even it out as it goes over the padding of the bulrush, so as not to have it look as if it bends. Tricky-ish. Make the head quite fat too.

Cover the padding of the beak, using long straight stitches the whole length of the beak in two strands of 612. You may find that you have to couch these long strands down with a little stitch or two, to keep them in place. Do so with tiny stitches in the same colour, crossing the long strands in such a way as to be more or less invisible. Do the same for the black line down the middle of the beak, using two strands of 310, likewise for the black tip of the beak. Add the orange bits on the lower half of the beak in two strands of 301. Have a look at the photograph to guide you. You may have to fiddle around a bit to make this beak look good, it's not all that easy, what with all the padding underneath it and its own padding. Take your time and it'll come out all right in the end.

Now do the orange patch under the eye (G on the Key Diagram), using two strands of 301 in Stem stitch.

Do the white patch (H on the Key Diagram), using two strands of Ecru in Stem stitch.

Do the metallic blue strips (I on the Key Diagram). Alternate lines of Elizabeth Stuart Cord No. 27 (or DMC Stranded Cotton No. 796 if you don't have the metallic thread) with lines of Stem stitch using two strands of 924. The metallic thread should be done as described in the specific instructions for Using Metal Thread (p.40), using one strand of 924 for the couching thread. If you have substituted 796, just do ordinary Stem stitch.

Do the white throat (J on the Key Diagram), using two strands of Ecru in Stem stitch.

Do the bird's back (K on the Key Diagram), using two strands of 932 in Stem stitch.

Now do the tough bit: covering the padding of the bird's head. Use Elizabeth Stuart Cord No. 27, just as for the cheek stripe, but not alternating with the 924 this time. It takes ages and is worth every second. If you are not using the metallic thread, use two strands of the 796 in Roumanian Couching. This is certainly a lot easier (and cheaper) and will do fine as an alternative.

The wing is pretty tricky, too. Outline all the little wing feathers, except those indicated by the L on the Key Diagram, using the metallic thread again, couched as before with one strand of 924. If you are not using the metallic thread, use one strand of the 796 couched down with the same. Either way, it's dreadfully fiddly but, if you use the metallic thread, will add a bit of glitter and if you're not, well, the poor little feathers have to be outlined anyway, don't they?

Fill in the little feathers shaded with dots on the Key Diagram, using one strand of 792 mixed with one strand of 932 in little slanting Satin stitch.

Fill in the unshaded, longer feathers indicated by the L on the diagram, using one strand of 792 in tiny Stem stitch. Fill in with one strand of 932 in tiny Stem stitch.

Do the bird's tail feathers in one strand of 792, in rows of tiny Stem stitch, with single lines of 932 to divide the feathers up.

Pad the orange breast of the bird using felt covered with bump or layers of bump on its own if you prefer.

Cover the breast padding with one strand of 301 mixed with two strands of 976 in Roumanian Couching.

Do the bird's little feet (I love these little feet, don't you?) using one strand of 310. Lay two little foundation strands the length of each toe and oversew them with tiny little stitches which will be raised slightly by the foundation stitches.

Otter

Outline the eye, nose and mouth, using one strand of 310 in tiny Stem stitch. Use one strand of Ecru to make a Chinese Knot for the highlight of the eye.

Pad the bits represented on the Key Diagram by the heavily outlined shaded areas. Make the otter really nice and fat. Use layers of felt covered with bump. See the specific instructions for Padding with Felt and Bump (p.39) which will remind you how to achieve a good contour round the thigh and front leg.

Now cover the grey and white bits of the face, chest and belly, represented on the Key Diagram by dotty shading. Use two strands of Ecru mixed with one strand of 646 in Roumanian Couching.

Do all the brown parts of the head, tail, body and legs, except for the left back leg (M on the Key Diagram) using one strand of 3031 mixed with two strands of 433, again in Roumanian Couching. You will have to leave the bit of tail that overlaps the border until later.

For the back left leg (M on the Key Diagram), fill in with three strands of 3031 in straight stitches.

Add the whisker 'dots' (well, what on earth are they called?) using one strand of 310 in tiny little stitches. Add the whiskers themselves, to look as if they grow out of the dots. For each whisker, just knot a single strand of Ecru, take it through the fabric from back to front and cut it off leaving about an inch and a half (3–4 cm) of whisker. You can trim them a bit shorter later. Have a look at the photograph to see where they go.

Do the little ear, using two strands of Ecru in a couple of tiny stitches.

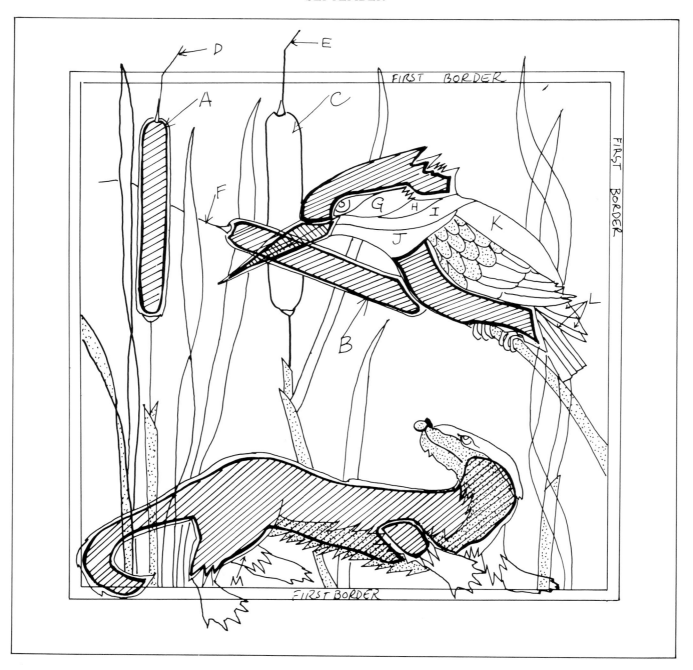

KEY DIAGRAM

You will have to leave the otter's feet until later.

Finish off the bits of bulrush leaf that cross over the otter's tail.

Borders

Do the first border in Satin Stitch Couching using four strands of bump for the padding, covered with three strands of 733.

Second: three strands of 310 in Stem stitch.

Third: Satin Stitch Couching using just two strands of bump for the padding and covering with three strands of 976.

Fourth: three strands of 932 in Stem stitch.

Fifth: If you have been using the Elizabeth Stuart metallic thread, you can now do a border in it. Cut off enough to go around all four sides of the border. Start at any corner. Lay the thread on the fabric, leaving about an inch (2–3 cm) spare to be taken through to the back, and couch the metallic thread down every quarter of an inch (½–1 cm) or so, using one strand of 924. Finish off as described in the specific instructions for Using Metal Thread (p.40).

If you haven't been using the metallic thread, ignore all that and do a border of Stem stitch using three strands of 796.

Sixth: Satin Stitch Couching, using four strands of bump for the padding, covered with three strands of 924.

Seventh: three strands of 932 in Stem stitch.

Eighth: Satin Stitch Couching, using four strands of bump for the padding, covered with three strands of 792.

Ninth: do the outside border in straight Satin stitch, using two strands of 301. Go around the outside edge first, with a foundation line of Stem stitch in any left over colour if you want to achieve a tidier outline. It's a bit of a bore, since your Satin stitches will cover this foundation line, but it does make it tidier.

Now you can finish off the otter's feet. Outline each foot using one strand of 310 in tiny Stem stitch. Do the toenails using one strand of Ecru. Make two or three tiny stitches in a 'V' shape for each nail.

Fill in the feet, toes and webs, using one strand of 646 in slanting Satin stitch.

Finish the two bulrush spikes that overlap the top border (one strand of 612 in Stem stitch).

Finish off the leaf tips that overlap the top border (two strands of 469 in Stem stitch).

Finish off the tail (one strand of 3031 mixed with two strands of 433).

Trim the whiskers if you think they need it (they might have got a bit bedraggled by now).

NUTHATCH · *Sitta europaea*
BADGER · *Meles meles*
HORSE CHESTNUT · *Aesculus hippocastanum*

October

I was in Oxfordshire not so long ago and driving late at night with some friends, when we saw this badger waddling down the middle of the road. It was such a lovely sight. He didn't seem to be in the least perturbed at being followed by a car and eventually sloped off into the undergrowth.

That's the only time I've ever been lucky enough to see a badger. I watched a programme on television once about a woman who put out food for badgers on her porch and between ten and twenty of them came almost every night for their supper! It really was the most amazing thing. That programme and my solitary Oxfordshire badger were enough to inspire me and make me want to include one of these gorgeous beasts somewhere amongst the pictures in this book. There was a ferocious fox sitting at the bottom of the horse chestnut tree originally, but I decided that he was rather unappealing and put the badger in his place. At least I've saved you the chore of doing all that Turkey Work that would have been involved in the fox's brush!

The badger is much easier to work than a fox would have been. He's the perfect chunky shape to pad easily, and the face is lovely to do.

I've seen nuthatches quite often. I love their turbo-streamlined look and beautiful colouring. I've put one on a tree in this typical nuthatch pose because I thought it was interesting that, according to some ornithological information I read, they are the only British birds who like going head first down trees; not a lot of people know that, to coin a phrase. They are called nuthatches because they wedge nuts in the bark and crack them open with the 'hatchet' beaks.

The horse chestnut leaves, like the poppies in the May chapter, have that wonderful way of catching the light at different angles so that they appear to have many more shades of autumn than the few I actually used. Embroidery is so beautiful.

I hope you will enjoy learning the Interlaced Chain Stitch. It looks so complicated and is actually so easy and effective. If you don't want to bother with it, don't worry. Simply fill in that border with another stitch you find easier.

The tree trunk is the best part of all. You can use any old stitch to build up a barky effect. Don't worry if your bark doesn't look like mine . . . it is, after all, a very stylized sort of a horse chestnut. That's the lovely thing about embroidery: if you were painting a picture of a tree you would probably feel obliged to be far more realistic, but with embroidery you can get away with murder by simply saying how 'stylized' you always intended it to be!

DETAILED OUTLINE

COLOURS YOU WILL NEED

(DMC Stranded Cotton, 1 skein of each unless otherwise stated)
No. 977 (orange)
No. 451 (light grey)
No. 413 (dark grey)
No. 932 (pale blue)
No. 733 (conker-shell green)
No. 833 (yellowy green)
No. 782 (golden brown)
No. 838 (dark brown)
No. 310 (black)
No. 3032 (beige)
No. 3051 (leaf green)
Ecru (cream)
Blanc neige (white)
Bump and Felt for padding

STITCHES YOU WILL NEED TO KNOW

Stem (p.35)
Satin (p.29)
Satin Stitch Couching (p.30)
Roumanian Couching (p.29)
Detached Overcast (p.23)
Interlaced Chain (p.24)
Chinese Knot (p.22)

GENERAL NOTES

I don't think that there are any really horrible things to contend with in this picture. The Interlaced Chain stitch is much easier than it looks and, if you don't already know how to do it, I think you will enjoy the learning process.

The tree looks as if it is going to be a nightmare, but is probably the easiest bit, just a matter of scattering little vertical, horizontal, wiggly, squiggly lines around with a smattering of Chinese Knots. Trace the Detailed Outline and transfer it on to your fabric as described in the chapter on General Know-How (p.17). Don't bother to trace any of the tree trunk detail, you can follow the photograph roughly, when you come to it. Don't trace the bird's feet, either, since these will be laid on top of the bark stitchery.

Use the colour photograph and the Key Diagram to help you follow the instructions.

The heavily outlined, shaded areas on the Key Diagram represent all the padded sections. Pad each section as you come to it in the instructions, using the specific instructions for Padding with Felt and Bump to help you (p.39).

Read the instructions for any stitches with which you are unfamiliar. Do use the right size and type of needle. It really does make a difference. See the chapter on General Know-How (p.17).

INSTRUCTIONS

Badger

Start with the badger's eyes. Outline in one strand of 310, using tiny Stem stitch. Fill in the pupils, again using one strand of 310 and filling the shape with tiny straight stitches. Add the highlight in each pupil, using one strand of Blanc neige in a Chinese Knot.

Still with the single strand of Blanc neige, go around the black outline of each eye with another outline in the white, again in tiny Stem stitch.

Fill in the whites of the eyes with one tiny stitch on each side of each pupil, again using one strand of Blanc neige.

Fill in the black muzzle using one strand of 310 in straight stitches and add the little nostrils on top, using one strand of 451 in tiny Stem or straight stitches.

Fill in all the white bits of the face, making neat rows of Stem stitch. Use one strand of Blanc neige to make a nice, tidy outline, but you can switch to two strands when you come to filling in the shape, to save a bit of time.

Add the little stitches in an upside down 'V' shape on the nose (C on the Key Diagram), using one strand of 451. Not of vital importance but, for some reason, these little stitches seem to lend a bit of expression to the badger.

Do the ears, again using two strands of Blanc neige. Lay four or five little stitches like half loops, the shape of the ear, fixing each one in place with a tiny couching stitch as you go along. These will pad the ears and raise them slightly from the black background. Now cover the foundation stitches with tiny overcast stitches.

Now you can fill in the black parts of the face. Again, you will find the edges to be neater if you first outline using just one strand of 310 and then fill in the less subtle bits with two strands, all in Stem stitch.

Body: pad the main bulk of the badger's body. Use layers of felt (you will need quite a few layers to make the body good and fat), covered with a layer of bump, as described in the specific instructions for Padding with Felt and Bump (p.39).

KEY DIAGRAM

Now cover this whole padded section with Roumanian Couching, using one strand of 413 mixed with one strand of 451 and one strand of Ecru. Look at the Detailed Outline to remind you of exactly where to go. Fill in the far front leg in this colour mixture (A on the Key Diagram), in Stem and little straight stitches, to fill the shape.

Fill in the darker legs, chest and underbelly (B on the Key Diagram), using one strand of 310 mixed with one strand of 413, working long-ish, shaggy sort of Stem-cum-straight stitches to fill in all the scraggy shaggy fur.

Do the little claws, using one strand of Blanc neige in a couple of tiny straight stitches for each claw. You will have to leave the one which overlaps the border until later.

Nuthatch

Outline the eye and fill in the pupil, just as you did for the badger, using one strand of 310 in tiny Stem stitch. Fill in the whites of the eye using one strand of Blanc neige in tiny straight stitches and make a single Chinese Knot, again in the single strand of white, for the highlight of the pupil.

Outline the beak, using one strand of 310 in tiny Stem stitch.

Outline the eye a second time, using one strand of 451 in tiny Stem stitch. Fill in the beak, again using one strand of 451, in little straight stitches.

Fill in the black stripe around the eye, using one strand of 310 in Stem stitch.

Now pad the areas of the head, throat and breast (represented on the Key Diagram by the heavily outlined, shaded sections), using layers of bump.

Cover the padding of the throat section (D on the Key Diagram), using two strands of Ecru in Roumanian Couching. Fill the orangey breast (E on the Key Diagram), using one strand of Ecru mixed with one strand of 977 in Roumanian Couching.

Outline all the tiny little wing feathers (no, I haven't forgotten the top of the head . . .) using one strand of 413 for the shorter, pale feathers (have a look at the photograph to see exactly which ones), in tiny Stem stitch.

Now you can go back to the top of the head and cover it and all of section F on the Key Diagram, into the little scallop shapes of the first row of feathers, using one strand of 451 mixed with one strand of 932 in Roumanian Couching.

Work the next row of feathers in the same colour mixture, but using slanting Satin stitch.

Fill in the longer wing feathers with one strand of 413 in tiny Stem stitches with lines of 3032 at intervals, to differentiate between the feathers.

For the tail feathers, use one strand of 413 to outline all the tail feathers in tiny Stem stitch and to fill in the sections shaded in black on the Key Diagram.

Fill in the centre feather (G on the Key Diagram) using one strand of 932 mixed with one strand of 451, in slanting Satin stitches, following the direction of the little lines on the Detailed Outline.

Use one strand of Blanc neige for the tiny little bits of white (have a look at the photograph . . . they really are very small), in tiny slanting Satin stitch.

Fill in any remaining bits of tail feather using one strand of 451 in more tiny little slanting Satin stitches.

And all I can add to that tail section is that I think it took longer to write than to sew. Phew!

Leave the bird's feet until later.

Leaves

Don't do the parts of the leaves that overlap the borders until later. You can draw all the veins on to your fabric first, if you want to. I personally found it easier to do them as I went along, without guidelines which never seemed to fall at exactly the right angle when I reached them with the background colour . . . see how you feel. I think you will understand what I'm talking about when you start working them. For all those leaves marked on the Key Diagram with a * , use one strand of 833 for the veins and one strand of 3051 for the rest, all in tiny Stem stitch rows.

Do the little curled section, H on the Key Diagram, in one strand of 3032, again in tiny Stem stitch rows, following the direction of the lines on the Detailed Outline.

Fill in all the golden brown leaves using one strand of 3032 for the veins and one strand of 782 for the rest, again all in tiny Stem stitch rows.

For the curled sections of the three leaves at the bottom of the picture, use one strand of 3032 in Stem stitch rows following the direction of the lines on the Detailed Outline.

For the last leaf at the bottom (I on the Key Diagram), use one strand of 3032 for the veins and one strand of 833 for the rest, all in tiny Stem stitch.

Conkers

Fill in the bits of dark brown showing on the top, split conker, using two strands of 838 in little Satin stitches.

Pad each shell section of this split conker, using bump.

Pad the other two conkers, using felt and bump or bump on its own.

Cover the brown section of the fallen conker (J on the Key Diagram), using two strands of 838 in Roumanian Couching.

Do a line of tiny little stitches between this brown section and the shell, using two strands of 3032.

Cover the shell section of this and the other two conkers, using two strands of 733, in Satin stitch for the split conker at the top and Roumanian Couching for the others.

Add the little spikes on each of the conkers, using two strands of 733 in a couple of little straight stitches for each spike.

Add the brown crack line on the top conker (K on the Key Diagram), using one strand of 838 in tiny Stem stitch.

Tree Trunk

This bit is really quite fun to do. You will find it easier to make it up more or less as you go along.

Basically, what I have done is to make a sort of mixture of scraggy little straight stitches, Chinese Knots, little detached chain stitches, tiny horizontal and vertical lines, and so on. You can use any stitch you happen to know that will give a rough bark-look.

I used the following colours: 833, 451, 413 and 3032. Mix one strand of 413 with one strand of 3032 for the darker, shady areas. Mix one strand of 833 with one strand of 451 for some of the Chinese Knots.

And so on. You can follow roughly what I've done by having a look at the photograph, but don't bother to be too exact, just have a bit of fun.

Do the little bits of branch (shaded in dots on the Key Diagram), using three strands of 3032 in Satin stitch padded out with a few long foundation stitches for each bit of branch.

Bird's Feet

Use one strand of 3032 mixed with one strand of 413 in Detached Overcast.

Use one strand of 310 in tiny little straight stitches for the claws.

I must say that I personally find Detached Overcast to be a dreadfully fiddlesome and irritating stitch, but the end result makes up for it. I stopped in between working each toe and had a quick scream and made a cup of very strong tea, but you may be more patient. I suppose we all have our favourite and unfavourite stitches and you might just adore this one.

Borders

The most sensible thing is to work the Interlaced Chain border first. You would find that, were you to work the actual first (brown) border before doing the chain, you would give yourself a ghastly job of avoiding the brown border with your needle when you came to the interlacing stitches . . . so, Interlaced Chain first.

This really is one of my favourite stitches.

Treat each side of the frame as an individual line. Make lines of chain stitch along the centre of the band (represented by the broken lines on the Detailed Outline), using three strands of 977. For the interlacing, use three strands of 932. Change to a blunt-ended tapestry needle. Cut off enough thread to make it from the top of one of the chain stitch lines (L on the Key Diagram) to the bottom (M of the Key Diagram). I found that this actually meant using about four times the actual length of the line, which seems a lot of thread to have in your needle at one time, but saves you panicking that you are going to run out of thread before you get to the end. It would be awfully tricky to have to start a new thread in the middle of a line of interlacing. You will find that you waste rather a lot of thread, but I think it's preferable to having a nervous collapse.

Do the interlacing down the other side in the same way.

Now work the line from point N on the Key Diagram, to point O. I found it helped to turn the fabric around in the embroidery ring so that I was working vertically, so to speak. It's up to you.

Do the last two sides of the square in the same way.

Now go back to the first, innermost border, marked FIRST BORDER on the Key Diagram. Use Satin Stitch Couching, with four strands of bump for the padding, covered with three strands of 838.

Now work the border on the other side of the Interlaced Chain, which we will call the third border. Use three strands of 413 in Stem stitch, taking care not to crowd the interlacing of the chain.

112

Fourth: Satin Stitch Couching using just three strands of bump for the padding, covered with two strands of Blanc neige.

Fifth: three strands of 782 in Stem stitch.

Sixth: finish with a border of straight Satin stitch, using two strands of 833 for the left and right sides and two strands of 733 for the top and bottom. If you want to achieve a neater finish, do a foundation line of Stem stitch along the whole outside edge first, using two strands of any left over colour (save your remaining 833 and 733 for the Satin stitches, I don't want you to run out).

Now you can finish any of the overlapping leaves, as described in the Leaves instructions.

Last of all, please don't forget the vitally important badger's claw which overlaps the border! Use one strand of Ecru and make two tiny stitches.

LONG-TAILED TITS · *Aegithalos caudatus*
WESTERN HEDGEHOGS · *Erinaceus europaeus*

November

I got the idea for using Bullion Knots for the hedgehogs from one of my very favourite embroidery books, Mrs Archibald Christie's *Samplers and Stitches*, which first appeared in 1920 and is still one of the best embroidery books I've seen, full of lovely ideas. Batsford publish it in paperback and I really do recommend it.

So, thank you Mrs Christie, for solving the problem of what stitch to use for hedgehogs. I must admit by about halfway through trying to learn this rather fiddly stitch I was thanking Mrs Christie somewhat less enthusiastically; it is a bit of a brute at first, but you soon learn how to sort out the messy bits with the tip of your needle and gritted teeth. The end result is miraculously hedgehoggy, so bear with me for asking you to do so many Bullion Knots.

The long-tailed tits are comparatively easy to work. The feathers look complicated, but are not terribly difficult to do, although you might find them a bit fiddly. I love the pink, black and white colour scheme of these little birds and I like the way the hedgehog on the left has obviously been woken up by their chattering and is extremely grumpy about the rude interruption of his hibernating plans. I do wish long-tailed tits visited townies like me; I get lots of blue and great tits, the occasional robin and even a jay or two, but I know that long-tailed tits don't frequent balconies in Central London.

The leaves are the most enjoyable part of the picture to work. You can really have fun here. You don't have to follow my suggestions if you know other stitches that would be good for leaves, such as Van Dyke or Cretan. Use a different stitch for each leaf if you know lots. Stick more or less to my colour scheme if you want a nice, autumnal look, but add more leaves if you want to, overlapping the borders or going further up the sides. Your hedgehogs could be even more smothered than mine, especially if you really hate the Bullion Knotting. Simply cover up more of the hedgehogs with leaves . . . I do love making life easier if I possibly can! In fact, if I'd thought of it when I designed the picture in the first place, I should have probably done just that, but anyway, see how you feel.

DETAILED OUTLINE

COLOURS YOU WILL NEED

(DMC Stranded Cotton, 1 skein of each unless otherwise stated)
No. 224 (pink)
No. 950 (pinky beige)
No. 830 (greenish brown)
No. 920 (rusty orange)
No. 838 (dark brown)
No. 451 (grey)
No. 436 (yellow)
No. 310 (black) 2 skeins
Ecru (cream)
Bump and Felt for padding

STITCHES YOU WILL NEED TO KNOW

Stem (p.35)
Satin (p.29)
Portuguese Knotted Stem (p.26)
Roumanian Couching (p.29)
Satin Stitch Couching (p.30)
Raised Fishbone (p.27)
Semi-Detached Buttonhole (p.31)
Bullion Knot (p.21)
Chinese Knot (p.22)

GENERAL NOTES

Don't panic at the thought of all those different stitches, and give up before you've started. I absolutely promise you that I didn't know most of them before I began work on this book. I think I'd done a bit of Stem and Satin stitch before, but all the others were completely new to me. Learning new stitches is really quite fun and I'm confident that, with the help of my brilliant instructions . . .well, I really have tried hard to make the process painless . . .you will enjoy working on this picture.

Trace the Detailed Outline and transfer it onto your fabric as described in the chapter on General Know-How (p.17).

Use the colour photograph and the Key Diagram to help you follow the instructions.

The heavily outlined, shaded sections on the Key Diagram represent all the areas to be padded. Pad each bit as you come to it in the instructions, using the specific instructions for Padding with Felt and Bump to help you (p.39).

Read the instructions for any stitches with which you are unfamiliar. Do use the right size and type of needle. It really does make a difference. See the chapter on General Know-How (p.17).

INSTRUCTIONS

Branch and First Border

Start at point A on the Key Diagram. Use one strand of 830 mixed with one strand of 451 in Portuguese Knotted Stem stitch. I made just a single knot around each of the Stem stitches . . . see the specific instructions for Portuguese Stem stitch (p.26) and you will see what I mean. Work your way in rows, up the right hand side from point A and turning off and along the branch at point B. Carry on along the branch, leaving gaps where the birds will be and doing the twiggy bits as you get to them. Finish at point C.

Now work your way up the left hand side of the first border, from point D to point E. At this stage I decided that I was desperately fed up with all those awful little knots, and carried on along the first border from point E back to point B in ordinary Stem stitch in the same colour scheme. You can do the whole lot in the Portuguese variety if you are a real devil for punishment, but don't feel guilty if you are sick and tired of it. I think the knobblyness of the knots is wonderful for the branch but really doesn't add much to the actual border bits. I only did D to E the hard way because at that stage I was still feeling guilty. It didn't last!

Whichever way you choose, when you come to the bottom border (between points A and D on the Key Diagram), most of which will eventually be covered with leaves, do use ordinary Stem stitch or you will find the knots getting horribly in the way of the leaf stitchery.

Long-tailed Tits

Do the long tails first. They are quite easy and quick to do and make you feel as if you're getting on well. Use three strands of 310 in slanting Satin stitches all the way along the length of each tail.

Use two strands of Ecru and fill in the white tail feathers, again using slanting Satin stitch.

Now outline the white tail feathers using one strand of 451 in tiny Stem stitch.

Now fill in the eyes and outline the beaks, using one strand of 310 in tiny little Stem and straight stitches. Fill in the beaks, using one strand of Ecru in little straight

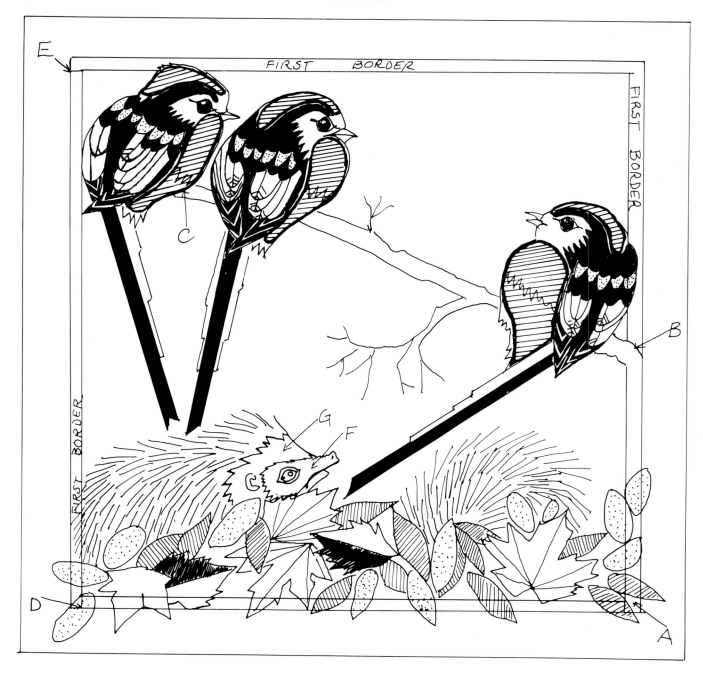

KEY DIAGRAM

stitches and make a single Chinese Knot in the centre of each pupil for the highlights, again using one strand of Ecru.

Now work all the rest of the black on all three birds. Fill in the stripes above the eyes, and their backs, using one strand of 310 in Stem stitch. Outline all the feathers the same way and add the few little black lines on the feathers.

Fill in the white parts of the birds' faces using one strand of Ecru in Stem stitch.

Fill in the white parts of the feathers again with one strand of Ecru, this time in slanting Satin stitches. Use the photograph to help you. Now fill in the little pink feathers (shaded with dots on the Key Diagram), using one strand of 950 mixed with one strand of 224 in Raised Fishbone stitch or little slanting Satin stitch if you can't face fiddling with fishbones in such small areas.

Now pad all the sections represented on the Key Diagram by the heavily outlined, shaded areas. Use bump and tiny bits of felt or bump on its own, whichever you prefer.

Cover the white, top sections of the breast and white tops of the heads, using two strands of Ecru in Roumanian Couching.

Cover the pink, lower sections of the breasts using one strand of 950 mixed with one strand of 224, again in Roumanian Couching.

Borders

Now go back to the merry task of wending your way cheerfully and good humouredly around all those borders. (You must understand that this was the eleventh picture that I had worked on in the space of about six months, so forgive me for the sarcasm. It's probably your first and you are still full of enthusiasm and I shouldn't put you off!) You have already done the first border as part of the branch. Ten out of ten if you stuck to the Portuguese Knotting most of the way round!

For the second border, use Satin Stitch Couching with two strands of bump for the padding, covered with three strands of 310.
Third: three strands of 224 in Stem stitch.
Fourth: three strands of 950 in Stem stitch.
Fifth: three strands of 920 in Stem stitch.
Sixth: three strands of 830 in Stem stitch.
Seventh: Satin Stitch Couching, using three strands of bump for the padding covered with three strands of 950.
Eighth: two strands of 451 in Stem stitch.
Ninth: finish up with a border of straight Satin stitch,

using two strands of 224. Lay a line of foundation Stem stitches all along the outside edge if you want to achieve a neater finish. Use any pale left over colour as it will be hidden by the Satin stitches eventually.

You don't have to work all these borders one after the other. You could take time off from the monotony of the slog around the edges to have a nervous collapse over the Bullion Knots of the hedgehogs, if you feel so inclined, or do some of the leaves that don't overlap your abandoned borders . . . see how you feel.

Hedgehogs

Left hand, un-curled hedgehog: Outline the mouth, do the nostril and fill in the pupil of the eye, using one strand of 310 in one tiny stitch for the nostril and tiny Stem stitch for the rest.

Outline the eye, using one strand of 451 in tiny Stem stitch.

Make a highlight in the pupil of the eye, using one strand of Ecru in a single Chinese Knot.

Fill in the grey area of the snout and around the eye (section F on the Key Diagram) using one strand of 451 in little straight stitches. Fill in the rest of the face (section G on the Key Diagram), using one strand of 436 mixed with one strand of 828 in spikey straight stitches. Add the little ear, using one strand of 838 in tiny stitches laid over a few foundation stitches, to pad the ear out a little bit.

Quills: or are they spines? I'm not sure . . . porcupines have quills, but do hedgehogs? Never mind. Make Bullion Knots for each one of the quills (or whatever they are). Make some of them in four strands of 838 mixed with two strands of Ecru. Make some in four strands of 310 mixed with two strands of Ecru. Pack the Bullion Knots closely together, more or less alternating the two colour schemes.

Bullion Knots are quite tricky to get used to but don't feel you have to be fantastically, perfectly neat. Take your time. They can get horribly tangly, but you will get better at sorting out the tangles as you go along, or maybe I'm the only one who can manage to make a pig's ear out of a hedgehog's quills/spines.

Work the Bullion Knots more or less in the directions of the little lines on the Key Diagram.

Where the hedgehog overlaps the border, do just that with the Knots.

Do the curled-up hedgehog in exactly the same colour scheme of Bullion Knots, again following the direction of the little lines on the Key Diagram.

Leaves

This is the reward for getting through the pricklyness of the hedgehogs' . . . prickles . . . is that what they are?

The leaves are really enjoyable to work, even when you're on your eleventh picture as I was!

Use Raised Fishbone for all those shaded with little lines on the Key Diagram, in one strand of either 920, 830 or 436. Have a look at the photograph if you want to follow my colour scheme exactly, although it really isn't essential.

Use Semi-Detached Buttonhole in two strands of any of those same three colours for all the leaves shaded with little dots on the Key Diagram.

I've rung the changes, as you can see from the photograph, with some in green edged with red or vice versa, some in green edged with yellow, some all yellow or all green or all red, some in half of one colour and half of another. See the specific instructions for Semi-Detached Buttonhole (p.31) to help you and, above all, have fun.

The leaves half shaded on the diagram with one dark side are done in slanting Satin stitch, one half in the yellow and the other in the green, using one strand of 436 or 830.

All the remaining big leaves are filled in with one strand of slanting Satin stitch and have veins worked over them in a contrasting colour. Again, look at the photograph if you want to follow my example or just do what you think works best. It couldn't matter less if your leaves are different from mine; just stick roughly to the autumnal colour scheme and enjoy yourself.

Fill in all the gaps between the leaves using one strand of 310 in little straight stitches.

December

The last one! It may be the first for you, but I can tell you that it was the culmination of months and months and months of stitching and stitching and stitching for me. When I began to work my way along that first December border and branch, I felt a real sense of achievement, knowing that I was nearly through working twelve embroideries. I've enjoyed it all but I must admit that none was quite such fun as the December picture.

I had a few tantrums trying to learn a hateful stitch called a Turk's Head Knot, which you will see from the instructions I abandoned pretty sharpish in favour of my easy way out. I really don't see the point in making one's life a misery over something like embroidery, which should be a relaxing occupation.

I'd rather dreaded the Christmas robins, not realising how I'd come to love the little dears as they represented the end in sight to all my labours, and I eventually came to like this design as much as any of the others. There wasn't much choice as to which bird should represent December. It could hardly have been anything but a robin, could it. I wanted to get away from the solitary Christmas card robin image, but as they are such pugnacious little brutes, if I was going to have two of them in a picture, they more or less had to be arguing about something. I don't suppose they like holly berries much, but they love a good fight, and a holly berry is as good an excuse as any.

I love the shiny spikyness of the holly leaves, and the way that the light catches them at different angles. They appear to be made up of far more shades of green than the two that I used, such is the beauty of embroidery.

This is quite an easy picture to work. Finding your way around the Key Diagram is the most difficult part of it all, I think! Don't feel obliged to follow all my border stitch suggestions; I've kept them fairly simple, as with all these pictures, but if you know other line stitches, do feel free to substitute them, but don't forget that different stitches use up different amounts of thread, and you may find that you will need more than I have allowed for.

ROBINS · *Erithacus rubecula*
HOLLY · *Ilex aquifolium*

122

COLOURS YOU WILL NEED

(DMC Stranded Cotton, 1 skein of each unless otherwise stated)
No. 451 (grey)
No. 731 (olive green)
No. 895 (dark holly-leaf green)
No. 3051 (sludgy branch-green)
No. 3032 (beige)
No. 3031 (dark brown)
No. 817 (holly berry red)
No. 301 (robin breast red)
Ecru (cream)
1 spool of Silver Divisible (DMC ref. no: D283). You won't need much, just enough to do the icicles, if you've got any left overs.

You will need a tiny amount of black for the robins' eyes and to outline the beaks. Use one strand of 310 if you have any lying around or you can get away with ordinary black cotton if you don't want to buy a whole new skein.
Bump and Felt for padding.

STITCHES YOU WILL NEED TO KNOW

Stem (p.35)
Satin (p.29)
Satin Stitch Couching (p.30)
Roumanian Couching (p.29)
Detached Overcast (p.23)
Raised Fishbone (p.27)
Chinese Knot (p.22)

GENERAL NOTES

Trace the Detailed Outline and transfer it onto your fabric as described in the chapter on General Know-How (p.17), but don't draw in the little cherry-stalks (the pen marks would show up under the Detached Overcast stitches) or the legs of the robins (the padding will cover your guidelines).

Use the colour photograph and the Key Diagram to help you follow the instructions.

The heavily outlined, shaded areas on the Key Diagram represent the padded sections. Pad each section as you come to it in the instructions, using the specific instructions for Padding with Felt and Bump to help you (p.39).

Read the instructions for any stitches with which you are unfamiliar. Do use the right size and type of needle. It really does make a difference. See the chapter on General Know-How. (p.17).

INSTRUCTIONS

Branches and First Border

Begin with all of the branches and first border. Use the Key Diagram to help you. I know it all seems rather complicated, but actually it's easier to sew than it was to explain, hence the wordiness.

Mix one strand of 3031 with two strands of 3051.

Start at point A on the Key Diagram. Cut off four strands of bump, each long enough to reach comfortably from point A to point B.

Cover this padding with your 3032/3051 mixture, following the direction of the little arrows.

Do exactly the same from point C to point D (it's a case of Hunt the Letters on the Key Diagram, isn't it . . .). Thin the padding out until your branch is flat and unpadded by the time it reaches point D, so as not to make a horrible edge against the leaf.

Do the section from point E to point F, keeping this little bit fat all the way.

Do the section from point G to point H, carrying straight on along the bits that will later be overlapped by the robin's wing feathers and the holly leaf.

Do the section from point I to point J, again going straight on along the bit where the leaf will overlap.

Do the section along the bottom from point K to point L, going straight on along the bit where the holly berry will overlap.

Now fill in all the other little bits of branch between the leaves and leading to them. Don't pad these little bits.

Add the three little branch knots, shaded black on the Key Diagram. Use one strand of 3032 in little stitches laid on top of the branch stitches . . . not tremendously important but there they are so you might as well do them.

Snow

Pad each section of snow with layers of bump, packing the stitches of the top layer closely together so that the covering knots don't disappear in between them.

Now cover with Chinese Knots, using three strands of Ecru. It takes ages.

DETAILED OUTLINE

Robins

Fill in the pupil of each eye, using one strand of 310 or ordinary black cotton, in little straight stitches. Outline the beaks in the same thread, using tiny Stem stitch.

Outline the eyes and fill in the beaks, using one strand of 451 in tiny Stem stitches.

Add the highlight in each pupil using one strand of Ecru in a single Chinese Knot.

Do the feet next. You will have to work round the feet later, which might seem a bit peculiar, but it's less tricky than trying to work Detached Overcast with a lot of padding in the way of your needle.

Use one strand of 3032 mixed with two strands of 3031, in Detached Overcast. Lay foundation stitches for the toes that form loops to make each toe curl around the branch. You don't need to detach the overcast stitches for the legs.

Now do all the padding of the robins, represented by the heavily outlined, shaded areas on the Key Diagram. Use felt covered with a layer of bump, or bump on its own.

Cover all the red sections of the breast and head and the unpadded 'cheek' bits and around the eyes, using two strands of 301 in Roumanian Couching. Fill in the little bits of red breast under the right hand bird's feet. Tricky, but not impossible. You can sort of push the toes about a bit to get in between them.

Cover the brown crown of the right hand bird's head and the crown and back of the left hand bird (the sections marked M on the Key Diagram), using one strand of 3031 mixed with one strand of 433, again in Roumanian Couching.

Do the white parts of the breasts, using two strands of Ecru, again in Roumanian Couching. Again, it's a bit tricky working your way around the feet of the right hand bird, but not impossible.

Fill in the tiny little grey patches on both birds (N on the Key Diagram), using two strands of 451 in little straight stitches.

Now outline all the wing and tail feathers, using one strand of 451 in tiny Stem stitch for the short feathers. For the longer wing feathers and the very long tail feathers of the left hand bird, use straight stitches laid the length of the line and kept in place by tiny, couching stitches at intervals along the line.

Overlap the border with the tips of the right hand bird's wing.

Fill in all the wing feathers using one strand of 451 mixed with one strand of 3031 in little straight or Stem stitches.

Fill in the bit of tail showing on the right hand bird in the same way.

Fill in the tail of the left hand bird in the same colour mixture, but do the central feather (O on the Key Diagram) in Raised Fishbone and the outside feathers in slanting Satin stitch, following the direction of the shading lines on the Key Diagram.

Borders

You have already done the first border when you did the branch sections.

You will have to stop and start at the snow mound until you have got past the fifth border.

Second: three strands of 433 in Stem stitch.

Third: three strands of 895 in Stem stitch.

Fourth: Satin Stitch Couching, using four strands of bump for the padding, covered with three strands of 817. This is the trickiest when it comes to negotiating the snow mound. Start on the right hand side of the snow mound and work your way round the frame until you reach the left hand edge of the snow mound. Fill in any of the tiny amount of red showing in the middle of the mound with a few little cheating, unpadded stitches. No-one will notice.

Fifth: three strands of 895 in Stem stitch.

Sixth: Satin Stitch Couching, using five strands of bump for the padding, covered with three strands of 301.

Seventh: straight Satin stitch, using two strands of 731 for the top and bottom sides of the frame and two strands of 3051 for the left and right sides. Do a foundation line all along the outside edge, if you want to achieve a tidier finish, using any left over thread for which you will have no more need . . . not the greens for the leaves or the red for the berries.

Leaves

Outline every leaf, using one strand of 731 in tiny Stem stitch. Do the central veins of each leaf in the same way, adding a few extra tiny straight stitches where the veins widen when they join the stems on the two lower leaves. Overlap the borders where the leaves do so. Fill in the leaf marked on the Key Diagram with a * using one strand of 731. Fill in all the other leaves using one strand of 895. For all the leaves, use lovely, long, silky, slanting Satin stitch. Where the stitches are too long to lie flat safely, couch them down as you go along, with stitches long enough and slanted enough to be as invisible as possible. The leaves look so shiny and lovely, and catch the light so beautifully when they are finished.

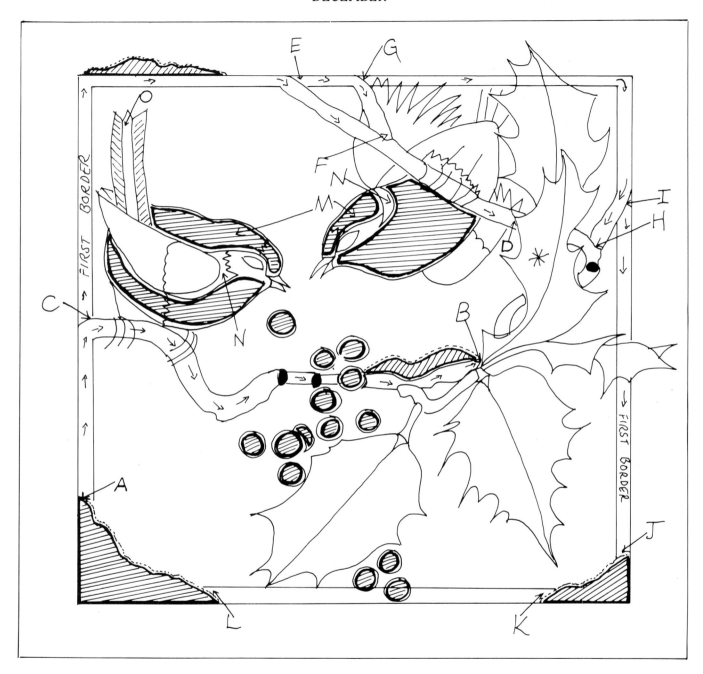

KEY DIAGRAM

Holly Berries

Do all the beastly little stalks first. Refer to the Detailed Outline or the photograph to remind yourself of where they go and don't worry if yours don't end up in exactly the same place as mine. It couldn't matter less and is much better than having horrible pen markings showing on the fabric underneath.

Use two strands of 3032 in Detached Overcast.

Don't be tempted to do the berries before you have finished all the stalks. It would be a nightmare trying to manoeuvre your Overcasting needle around amongst all that padding.

There are all sorts of brilliant ways of making bobbles and if you know one of them, do use your own technique. I personally felt like screaming and jumping off a cliff when I tried to get to grips with a Turk's Head Knot, for example, and opted for the easy way out. The experts will probably faint with horror but at least I haven't gone completely round the bend and I might have saved you, too, from total hysteria. Anyway, they are only really sort of half-bobbles and I don't think you can halve a Turk's Head. So, purists skip this bit . . . For each berry: cut a tiny, weeny little strip of felt and curl it up into a miniature snail. Skewer the snail in place, using one or two tiny stitches in three strands of 817. Cover this snail padding with the same three strands of 817, criss-crossing two and fro until no padding shows through. Voila! A half-bobble. Add the little dot on each berry, using two strands of 3031 in a single Chinese Knot.

Overlap the border with the berry at the bottom . . .you will need an even smaller snail to pad this one, and the little half covered berry in the middle.

Icicles

One last grizzly bit. Use one strand of the Silver Divisible. Separating this silver thread is really awful. Don't be too ambitious with the length you cut off, then it will be marginally easier.

For each icicle, lay a foundation stitch the length of the icicle and work back over it in tiny, slanting Satin stitches.

List of suppliers

There are many suppliers of needlework requirements. Big department stores often have good haberdashery and fabric departments but don't always stock the DMC yarns that I have used. Check by telephone if you are unsure.

The linen/cotton mix fabric that I used is available at Liberty in Regent Street, London W1, but more or less any even weave linen, heavy cotton or synthetic fabric will do. Look around the fabric departments of big stores, or you could even get away with a bit of old sheet, which is what I used for the little sampler pictures (see Introduction).

DMC will send you a list of suppliers nationwide of their range of yarns if you write to them enclosing a stamped addressed envelope to DMC Dunlicraft, Pullman Road, Wigston, Leicester LE8 2DY.

The following specialist shops stock DMC yarns and the Elizabeth Stuart metallic threads:

The Royal School of Needlework
5 King Street
Covent Garden
London WC2 8HN
(mail order only)

Simply Threads
At Colourway
112A Westbourne Grove
London W2 5RU
Tel: 01 229 1432
(shop and mail order)

The Campden Needlework Centre
High Street
Chipping Campden
Gloucestershire GL55 6AG
Tel. 0386 840 583
(shop and mail order)

Pomegranates
East Street
Petworth
West Sussex GU28 0AB
Tel: 0798 42688
(shop and mail order)

Christine Riley
53 Barclay Street
Stonehaven
Kincardineshire
Scotland AB3 2AR
Tel: 0569 63238
(shop and mail order)

The Spinning Jenny
Bradley
Keighley
W. Yorkshire BD20 9DD
Tel: 0535 32469
(shop and mail order)